D1141710

WITHDRAWN

WITHDRAWN

The Language of Colour

The Language of Colour provides a fresh and innovative approach to the study of colour from the co-author of the best-selling textbook, *Reading Images*.

Moving on from the meanings of single colours, Theo van Leeuwen develops the theory that many different features shape the way we attach meaning to the colours we see in front of us, and the idea that colour schemes are more important than individual colours. Chapter topics include:

- a brief history of the meanings of colour

- the relationship between language and colour names within a cultural context

- corporate uses of colour

- the meaning of colour in everyday life.

Spanning a wide range of examples from graphic design to the visual arts, this title presents a cutting-edge and engaging overview of the use of colour in a wide variety of situations and cultural and historical contexts. Incorporating both contemporary and traditional theory and supplemented by questions and ideas for projects at the end of every chapter, *The Language of Colour* is the ideal textbook for students of multimodality and language and communication within applied linguistics, communication studies, art and design and cultural studies.

Theo van Leeuwen is Dean of the Faculty of Arts and Social Sciences at the University of Technology, Sydney. He is author of numerous titles, including *An Introduction to Social Semiotics* (2005), *Reading Images* (second edition, 2006) with Gunther Kress, and *The Language of New Media Design* (2008) with Radan Martinec, all published by Routledge.

'Theo van Leeuwen is one of the master teachers of visual communication, and his new book, *The Language of Colour*, goes beyond the usual sources in history and psychology to propose a social semiotics of color, providing concrete examples and exercises to dazzle the eye and the mind.'

Kevin G. Barnhurst, *University of Illinois at Chicago, USA*

'Now more than ever colour is playing a central role in everyday communication and, with this book, at long last we have a systematic method for analyzing how people use colour for cultural expression and social communication. The framework presented here takes us beyond traditional approaches that simplistically map colour to meaning, to a perspective that helps us to understand the socially situated and material aspects of colour as a semiotic mode. This book will be of great interest to students in a variety of disciplines from design to discourse analysis, as well as anyone else interested in the ways we make meaning in our increasingly "technicolour" world'

Rodney Jones, *City University of Hong Kong*

The Language of Colour

An introduction

Theo van Leeuwen

LIS LIBRARY	
Date	Fund
16/6/12	1-che
Order No	
2326231	
University of Chester	

Routledge
Taylor & Francis Group

LONDON AND NEW YORK

First published 2011
by Routledge
2 Park Square, Milton Park, Abingdon, Oxon OX14 4RN

Simultaneously published in the USA and Canada
by Routledge
270 Madison Ave, New York, NY 10016

Routledge is an imprint of the Taylor & Francis Group, an informa business

© 2011 Theo van Leeuwen

The right of Theo van Leeuwen to be identified as author of this work has been
asserted by him in accordance with sections 77 and 78 of the Copyright, Designs
and Patents Act 1988.

Typeset in Helvetica by
Swales & Willis Ltd, Exeter, Devon
Printed and bound in Great Britain by
TJ International Ltd, Padstow, Cornwall

All rights reserved. No part of this book may be reprinted or reproduced or utilized in
any form or by any electronic, mechanical, or other means, now known or hereafter
invented, including photocopying and recording, or in any information storage or
retrieval system, without permission in writing from the publishers.

British Library Cataloguing in Publication Data
A catalogue record for this book is available from the British Library

Library of Congress Cataloging in Publication Data
Van Leeuwen, Theo, 1947–
The language of colour : an introduction / Theo van Leeuwen. — 1st ed.
    p. cm.
    1. Language and color. I. Title.
    P120.C65L44 2011
    302.2 — dc22   2010027594

ISBN13: 978–0–415–49537–0 (hbk)
ISBN13: 978–0–415–49538–7 (pbk)

Contents

Contents

Illustrations

The following illustrations appear in a colour plate section between pp. 52 and 53.

Preface

I had already taught and written about visual communication for more than a decade when I began to realize how little I had to say about colour. I soon realized I had blindly followed an age-old prejudice for 'design' over colour. Even art historians have often discussed works of art with hardly a mention of colour.

Such realizations do not come from nowhere. In the world around me, colour had made a comeback. The media I had been teaching about at Macquarie University and the London College of Printing – the press, television, film – had all moved to colour, though few media and film theorists had paid serious attention to it. Then colour, aided by new computer software, entered the world of what formerly had been austere, type-written documents and lecture overhead slides. It was time to pay attention. My students were asking questions about it. And I did not have many answers.

I began to read my way into the subject, discovering how little has been added to colour theory since the heady years of De Stijl and Bauhaus, though philosophers have of course always written about colour, and though theorists such as Barthes, Kristeva and Derrida had, more recently, heralded the return of colour, praising it as subversive, pleasureful, and 'escaping the inky law of the trace' (Derrida, 1987: 172). My most important discovery was the work of John Gage, whose books *Colour and Culture* (1993) and *Colour and Meaning* (1999) cover almost every aspect of the theory and practice of colour and brought home that there is no single 'language of colour', whatever the psychologists say, but that colour has been used, and theorized, in many different ways. I had already begun to embed semiotic analysis in social and cultural history in earlier work, but reading Gage spurred me on to move even further in this direction. I will never be able to equal the depth of his knowledge, the result of a lifetime of study of colour, and the influence of his work can be felt on almost every page of this book.

It is equally important to acknowledge the contribution of my long-time and ever inspiring collaborator Gunther Kress. The theory of colour presented in this book was developed in a series of conversations with Gunther, based on the work we published in our book *Multimodal Discourse* (2001), and first published in an article called 'Colour as a semiotic mode: notes towards a grammar of colour' (Kress and Van Leeuwen, 2002). Again, there is not a page in this book in which the influence of Gunther's originality and sense of intellectual direction cannot be felt. I am also grateful to David Machin and Emilia Djonov for inspiring discussions on the subject, and to Kate Belsey for allowing me to teach two semester-long seminars on colour to students of Cardiff University's Critical and Cultural Theory Centre – my students in these seminars have contributed more to clarifying and organizing my ideas about colour than they are probably aware of.

This book is, again, written for students and I am grateful to my editor, Louise Semlyen, for continuing to publish the kind of textbooks I write – books which are at once an exploration of new ideas, or at least a new synthesis of ideas, and written for students. Writing for students means, to me, writing as clearly as possible, but without any form of condescension, and modelling, in the form of the 'exercises' which conclude each chapter, how to read the literature closely and carefully, how to critically analyse examples, and how to explore colour by actually using it, and I very much hope that this book will turn out to be useful for students of the theory as well as the practice of colour.

I would also like to thank my employer, UTS, for generously allowing me a period of study leave in the middle of a contract as Faculty Dean, and Geoff Riordan for taking over from me during my absence. Without this contribution, the book could not have been written. Finally I would like to thank Sophie Jaques for her work in chasing picture permissions and Deborah Bateson for moral support and a wonderful home environment in which to get on with the hard work of actually getting the book on paper.

Theo van Leeuwen, March 2010

Acknowledgements

Every effort has been made to trace copyright holders and obtain permission. Any omissions brought to the attention of the publisher will be remedied at the earliest opportunity.

Figure 1.1 reproduced with permission from Xerox. Staff satisfaction survey from 1996.

Figures 3.1, 3.2, 3.4 and 3.8 reproduced by permission of Dumont Buchverlag, taken from *Schule der Farben Grundzüge der Farbentheorie für Computeranwender und andere* by Harald Küppers.

Figures 3.5, 5.5 and 5.6 by kind permission of David Hornung from *Colour – A Workshop for Artists and Designers* (2005).

Figure 3.10 El Greco, *Madonna and Child with Saint Martina and Saint Agnes* from the Widener Collection. Image courtesy of the Board of Trustees, National Gallery of Art, Washington.

Figure 5.3 Rembrandt, *The Anatomy Lesson of Dr. Tulp* by permission of the Royal Picture Gallery Mauritshuis, The Hague.

Figure 5.6 by kind permission of Rachel Moore. *Arrows* 2003. rachey1982@hotmail.com

Figure 5.7 by kind permission of Clare Perkins.

Figure 6.1 Vincent van Gogh, *Le café de nuit* (The Night Café). Courtesy of Yale University Art Gallery. Bequest of Stephen Carlton Clark, B.A. 1903.

Figure 6.2 Paul Klee, *Static Dynamic Graduation*, 1923. Image copyright The Metropolitan Museum of Art/Art Resource/SCALA, Florence. © Photo SCALA, Florence.

Figure 6.3 Barnett Newman, *Onement I*, 1948. © 2010. Digital image, The Museum of Modern Art, New York/SCALA, Florence. With permission of The Barnett Newman Foundation.

Figure 6.4 Barnett Newman, *Who's Afraid of Red, Yellow and Blue II*. With permission of the Barnett Newman Foundation.

Figure 6.5 Le Corbusier, *Purist Still Life*. © ADAGP, Paris and DACS, London 2010.

Figure 6.6 Taken from R. Koolhaas, N. Foster and A. Mendini (2001) *Colours*, with permission of V&K Publishing.

Figure 7.1 © Colin Poole, with permission of PhotoWord Limited.

Figure 7.2 taken from E. Lupton, *Thinking with Type – A Critical Guide for Designers, Writers, Editors and Students* (2004). By permission of Princeton Architectural Press

Figure 7.4 Lynn S. Bickley, *Pocket Guide to Physical Examination and History Taking* (2009), by permission of Wolters Kluwer.

Figure 7.5 Colour scheme of the *South China Morning Post*. Designed by de Luxe & Associates.

1 Introduction

1.1 A social semiotics of colour

This book presents a social semiotics of colour – an account of the way society uses colour for purposes of expression and communication, whether in art, architecture, fashion, or everyday objects. It is therefore not in the first place about the natural science of colour, the physics of light or the science of colour perception, even though these subjects will be touched on if and when necessary. It is about the *social* science of colour. It is about the deliberate creation and use of dyes, pigments, stains, etc. and of devices for projecting and reflecting light, and about the way they are used to *manipulate* colour for the expression of feelings, for the communication of ideas, and for social interaction.

Social semiotics, as I understand it here, has three dimensions: (1) the study of *semiotic resources* and their histories; (2) the study of *semiotic practices*, of the uses of semiotic resources in specific social, cultural and historical contexts, together with the discursive practices that evaluate, teach, explain and control these uses; and (3) *semiotic change*, the exploration and development of new semiotic resources and new semiotic practices. I will discuss these in turn.

Looking at colour as a semiotic resource means, first of all, focusing on its materialities and technologies. Communicative and expressive uses of colour cannot exist without the manufacture of pigments and dyes. Prehistoric cave painters used yellow and red earth, white chalk, and a black made from the soot of animal fat. Over time, new colours were constantly invented, using a wide range of materials and processes. Chinese yellow (*gamboge*) was made from the resin of the *garcina* tree (Finlay, 2002: 244), Indian yellow from the urine of cows that had been fed mango leaves (Plümacher, 2007: 67), saffron from a flower, the *Crocus sativus*. In the Europe of the Middle Ages, red was made from kermes insects, but when the Spanish conquistadores returned from the Americas they brought not only gold, silver and new foodstuffs, but also a new red, made from cochineal beetles (Finlay, 2002: 124). Such colours were expensive. In ancient times more than 10,000 murex shellfish had to be crushed to make a single gram of purple, as a result of which purple became the colour of priests, kings and emperors in ancient Persia and Rome. In the Renaissance, patrons would contractually require painters to use expensive pigments to add value to the works they commissioned, for instance gold paint, or ultramarine, which was made from the semi-precious gemstone lapis lazuli that had to be imported from 'across the sea' ('*ultra marine*'). Later, chemists began to develop synthetic paints, often from metals such as cobalt (*cobalt blue*), zinc (*zinc white*) etc., adding many new colours to the vocabulary of the language of colour. Without these new colours (and the portable tubes they came in) Impressionism and other modern art movements would not have been possible. Today, still more pigments are invented, many of synthetic organic origin, adding new colours, greater transparency for mixing or glazing, greater 'lightfastness' and so on. Colour printing techniques and colour film and video also continue to improve, and modern software is, of course, the newest colour resource. Photoshop makes the colour manipulation of photographic images widely available. Word and PowerPoint allow colour to be added to documents which only yesterday were rigorously black and white. The number of colours computers can produce has quickly risen from 16 kinds of grey to millions of colours, more than anyone could possibly need.

But such new colours are not developed in a vacuum. They develop in response to new communicative and expressive needs. A good example is the rise of black as a colour for clothing in the sixteenth century. The Protestant Reformers of the period disapproved of vivid colours and favoured dark (and especially black) dress, to express the virtues of a sober and serious lifestyle. As a result, demand for black dye rose and dyers, looking for new materials and new processes, began to use logwood that had to be imported from the Caribbean. Paradoxically, as Finlay notes (2002: 107) 'the clothes of the most puritanical of Puritans were often made with a colour collected by rough retired pirates and paid for by exchange for rum and enough cash to keep several brothels busy on the Caribbean coast'.

But looking at colour as a semiotic resource not only means looking at colour technologies, it also means looking at the way colour *meanings* developed, looking at what people have 'said' and done with colour. The history of colour has gradually built up a large repertoire of possible colour meanings that continues to be available to us as a resource for communication and expression, and that is continually added to. Black, for instance (see Pastoureau, 2008), has not only developed to express severity and seriousness, in the context of early Protestantism, it has also been used as the colour of death and misadventure ('a black day'), of sin and dishonesty ('black market'), of provocation, hate and aggression ('blackshirts', black flags), of sadness ('a black mood'), of fear (e.g. in 'film noir'), of authority (policemen, guards etc.), and of elegance, opulence or modernity (the black tuxedo, the little black dress, the art-house film, the programme of a classical concert). Yes, perhaps black does inevitably and everywhere remind of darkness and the night, and yes, perhaps blacker blacks do so more intensely than greyer blacks. But even this is not black's only possible source of associations. Black can also gain meaning because, like white, it can be interpreted as *not* being a colour, as negating or suppressing the more extroverted emotionality of vivid colour, and therefore as 'restrained' or 'modest'. And its association with darkness can trigger a *range* of different associations – associations with fearful things that happen in the night (nightmares) as well as evil things 'that cannot bear the light of day'. Nor is black the only possible signifier for death. In China and Japan the colour of sickness and death is white. True, there is always a reason for why a given colour becomes associated with given feelings or ideas, but that does not mean there is an inescapable cause-and-effect relation between the idea that is being expressed and the colour that expresses it. The relation is always only partial. Another aspect of the same idea might lead to an association with another colour. Death can be black as well as white. Darkness can engender fear, but we can also pale with fear. In each case there *is* a link, a motivation, a reason connecting the signifier with the signified, yet the same signified can couple with different signifiers, and the same signifier with different signifieds. Without taking the context into account, the *practices* in which these feelings and meanings are embedded and the normative discourses that surround them, colour remains, if not entirely open to any interpretation, nevertheless pretty subjective, pretty wide open to interpretation, and words are needed to guarantee sufficient intersubjectivity, sufficient sharing of meaning for colour to do the social work it is meant to do, at least in its early stages, when new meanings and new uses of colour are established – later such meanings might come to be understood without any need for explanation.

This brings us to the second dimension of the social semiotics of colour, *colour practices*, the uses of colour in specific social contexts, whether today or in the past, and the ways in which such uses are, or were, discursively established and controlled. In his book about the colour black, Pastoureau (2008) has pointed out that black as a colour for dress became popular in the mid-fourteenth century among merchants who had accumulated great wealth, but were nevertheless denied access to the social status of the aristocracy. This innovation needed verbal reinforcement. As said, colour meanings are not necessarily understood naturally, without the aid of authoritative explanations. There is a need for normative discourses, whether they are informal or formal, authoritative and prescriptive or working with suggestion and 'best practice' advice (this will be discussed in more detail in Chapter 7). A 1430 treatise about colour defended black: 'Even though the colour black seems sad, it is of high standing and great virtue. That is why the merchants and rich bourgeois, men as well as women, are dressed and adorned in it . . . One sometimes even finds black fabrics of a price equal to that of precious scarlets' (quoted in Pastoureau, 2008: 100). Later, the Protestant Reformers not only explicitly instructed believers to wear black (or at least dark) clothes, but also explicitly explained what this was meant to express: humility and contrition (Adam and Eve had to cover their nakedness after they had sinned), simplicity and functionality. White ('innocence') was recommended for children, and sometimes for women. Blue was tolerated so long as it remained dark and subdued. Multicoloured clothes were condemned – they make 'men look like peacocks', said Melanchton in a 1527 sermon (quoted in Pastoureau, 2008: 132). In short, the meanings of the Protestant dress code were quite explicitly taught and enforced, quite explicitly controlled. But while new semiotic practices, in their early stages, need such explanation and confirmation, in due course they may become common-sense, apparently natural and self-evident – but only apparently. As Pastoureau has said (2008: 16):

> Colour is defined first of all as a social phenomenon. It is the society that 'makes' the colour, that gives it its definitions and meanings, that constructs its codes and values, that organizes its customs and determines its stakes.

Social semiotics, therefore, needs to take account both of what Pastoureau refers to as the 'codes', for instance the range of colours used in a given domain, and the meanings and associations attached to them in that domain, and of the cultural and historical *contexts* of the codes, the way they were created, introduced in society, and enforced or defended.

'Puritan' black was a major new practice in the history of Western colour semiotics, and its influence can still be felt today. Other practices might be more restricted or shortlived. Many contemporary children's toys are made of brightly coloured plastic. Books for very young children also tend to feature bright primary colours. The rationale for this was developed by early twentieth-century colour psychologists, in other words, by scientific rather than religious authorities. Jonas Cohn, for instance, writing in the 1890s, established that preference for strong, saturated colours is a basic human 'instinct', only later repressed by culture, and therefore strongly present in children (see Gage, 1999: 192). Educators, designers and manufacturers took up this idea as part of developing a new 'culture of childhood' with its own (more or less 'unisex') dress code, its own literature – and its own colour schemes. More recently the tide has swung back and children are introduced to adult culture much earlier, including strong gender differentiation. Consequently bright reds, yellows and blues have to some degree been replaced by more subdued and hybrid colours, with a preponderance of pinks and mauves and purples for girls. In modern toyshops you can see the two styles side by side. Traditional Lego blocks, for instance, still come in bright white, yellow, blue, red and green, but the Lego blocks in boxes for building Star Wars space crafts come in more realistic blues and metallic greys.

The third dimension of social semiotics is semiotic change, the development of new semiotic resources and new semiotic practices, not only by studying how and why new practices were introduced, or disappeared, in the past, but also by actively contributing to the process of semiotic change. By studying which resources and practices exist and which do not, semiotics can expose gaps and ask *why* certain kinds of colour, or certain uses of colour, do not exist. The philosopher Ludwig Wittgenstein (1978), like a good semiotician, constantly imagined colours and combinations of colours which the colour theory he read did not allow for. Why can't we conceive of a 'pure brown'?, he asked, or a 'deep white'? Why is there no 'luminous black'? Semiotics, as I hope this book will show, can develop ideas about 'purity', 'deepness' and so on that might help catalyse not only the answer to Wittgenstein's questions but also the creation of new colours. In the course of this book we will see just how often new ideas about colour have gone hand in hand with artistic innovation, and vice versa. The same applies to the uses of colour, for instance in children's toys. Is there an alternative to either the modernist 'unisex' approach or the new gendered colour codes? What would it be and how would it be configured in what kinds of toys? Answering such questions requires ideas about gender, as well as ideas about colour. Again, the most innovative artists have always engaged in theory as well as practice, practising their theories so as to create innovative works and theorizing their practices so as to help people understand the reasons for their innovations.

To sum up, a social semiotics of colour studies colour in three ways:

• It studies semiotic resources, asking what kind of colours have people created, and how have they used them for purposes of social communication and expression.

• It studies semiotic practices, asking how people, in specific contexts, *use* colour, how these uses of colour come about, and how are they propagated and justified.

• It contributes to the on-going development of the language of colour by creating new ways of thinking about colour and its uses, and by actively influencing colour practices.

1.2 Colour versus design

Philosophy is a good place to look for some background to the subject of this book, and to explore the key ideas about colour that shape – and are shaped by – the colour practices of contemporary art, design and everyday life. For some 2,500 years Western philosophers have struggled with the subject, often viewing colour as highly subjective and as 'excessive', in need of restraint and subjugation to a rational order. Colour has always been, and still is, a subject that evokes strong feelings. Pliny, who lived in the first century AD, criticized abundant colour and 'florid painting'. The great Greek painter Apelles, he said, used only four restrained, austere colours, a black called 'atramentum', a white from Milos, Attic yellow, and a red from Sinope in the Black Sea. This emphasis on the moral virtues of a limited number of 'pure' or 'primary' colours, ordered in terms of some rational scheme, runs like a thread through colour theory, from its earliest days. The pre-Socratic philosopher Democritus (fifth century BC) already recognized just four colours (white, black, red and 'chloron', a pale yellow-green) each related to a basic shape, an 'atom' (Democritus was the originator of the term 'atom', which means 'indivisible' in Greek), and Aristotle, as Newton would do later, recognized seven basic colours (white, black, red, yellow, brown, violet, green and blue), related by numerical regularities, and analogous to the octave in music. In Chapter 3, I will discuss the issue of 'primary colours' in more detail.

Renaissance artists and thinkers rediscovered and translated these ancient writings, and initiated the long debate between *disegno* and *colore*, design and colour. The Florentine painters favoured *disegno*, the Venetians *colore*. Florentine painters such as da Vinci and Michelangelo saw design as the essential aspect of artworks, the medium in which artworks are conceived, hence a creation of the mind. Colour they saw as secondary, at best enlivening the work, and appealing to the senses rather than the mind. *Chiaroscuro*, the subtle play of light and shade, took precedence over colour. As Alberti wrote in his 1435 treatise *On Painting*, white and black are 'the colours with which we express light and shade', while other colours are only 'the matter to which variations of light and shade can be applied' (quoted in Gage, 1995: 118). Leonardo da Vinci, too, preferred light and dark, avoiding abundant colour, and focusing on creating an illusion of reality rather than using colour to express symbolic meanings or revel in the beauties of brilliant colour, as had been common in the Middle Ages, when colours denoted theological virtues, characters from the Bible or the ranks of noblemen, and were also highly appreciated for their intrinsic beauty. In his *Treatise*, Leonardo recommended that painters should compare their colours directly to the colours of their subjects by holding sample painted on paper against the real scene 'so that the colour you make may coincide with the natural colour' (quoted in Gage, 1995: 136). The Florentine painters' relative lack of interest in colour was reflected in their practice. Just as architects do not themselves build the buildings they design, so these artists did not themselves paint their paintings, but produced a *grisaille*, a black and white version, leaving the colouring to their assistants.

The Venetian painters disagreed with this view. Although they did argue against the use of colour for its own sake, they advocated using colour to 'give relief to the figures'. In the words of Lodovice Dolce, a supporter of Titian (*ibid.*: 137):

> Let no one think that the power of colour consists in the choice of beautiful colours, like beautiful blues, beautiful greens and so on, since these colours are just as beautiful without being set to work, but rather it consists in knowing how to handle them appropriately. [Some painters] do not know how to imitate the different nuances of cloth, but put the colours on fully saturated as they stand, so that in their works there is nothing to praise but the colours.

Venetian painters used both line and colour in the design stage, starting the whole process with a small 'cartoon' in oil to work out the colour relationships. El Greco, who had worked in Venice, thought that colouring was far more difficult than drawing. Michelangelo, he said, 'was a fine chap but didn't know how to paint' (*ibid.*: 348).

Views such as these would later be enshrined in the works of key philosophers. Immanuel Kant's *Critique of Judgment*, published in 1790, was, and still is, a highly influential and often quoted statement of the primacy of design, focusing on two key themes. According to Kant, colour can, first of all, only be beautiful if it is pure and unmixed (Kant, 1978: 66):

> Sensations of colour as well as of tone are only entitled to be immediately regarded as beautiful where, in either case, they are pure . . . Composite colours do not have this advantage, because not being simple, there is no standard for estimating whether they should be called pure or impure.

In addition, colour is secondary, an embellishment, to be *subjugated* to line, and at best adding 'charm' (*ibid.*: 67):

> In painting, sculpture, and in fact in all the formative arts, in architecture and horticulture, so far as fine arts, the design is what is essential. Here it is not what gratifies to sensation, but merely what pleases by its form, that is the fundamental prerequisite for taste. The colours which give brilliancy to the sketch are part of the charm. They may no doubt, in their own way, enliven the object for sensation, but make it really worth looking at and beautiful they cannot. Indeed, more often than not the requirements of the beautiful form restrict them to a very narrow compass, and, even where charm is admitted, it is only this form that gives them a place of honour.

Design as rational, objective, and therefore morally superior – colour as subjective, emotive and therefore morally inferior, that was the core of the message. Many of the instructional writings used in nineteenth-century academies echoed Kant's view, e.g. Charles Blanc's influential 1879 *Grammar of the Arts of Drawing* (quoted in Riley, 1995: 6):

> The union of design and colour is necessary to beget painting just as the union of man and woman to beget mankind, but design must maintain its preponderance over colour. Otherwise painting speeds to its ruin: it will fall through colour just as mankind fell through Eve.

Other philosophers, however, began to give colour a more important role. Hegel, writing in the 1840s, *celebrated* the multiplicity, subjectivity and sensuousness of colour (Hegel, 1975: 848):

> The hither and thither of reflections and sheens of colour, this mutability and fluidity of transitions, is spread over the whole, with the clarity, the brilliance, the depth, the smooth and luscious lighting of colours, a pure appearance of animation and this is what constitutes the magic of colouring and is properly due to the spirit of the artist who is the magician.

More recently, poststructuralist writers have followed his example. Roland Barthes (1985: 203–4) wrote of colour as 'a challenge offered to the Aristotelian rules of structure' and 'a kind of bliss' (*ibid.:* 166):

> It suffices that colour appear, that it be there, that it be inscribed like a pinprick in the corner of the eye . . . It suffices that colour lacerate something: that it pass in front of the eye, like an apparition – or a disappearance, for colour is like a closing eyelid, a tiny fainting spell.

Jacques Derrida (1987: 172), like Kant, set line (the 'trait', in his terminology) against colour. But he reversed the values. The 'rigour' of the 'incisive' and 'definite' 'law' of the line was now on the negative side of the equation, and the 'transgressive', 'gushy', 'violent' 'wash of colour' on the positive side, in a homage to the power of colour that is even more lyrical than that of Barthes:

> The rigour of the divide between the trait and colour becomes more trenchant, strict, severe and jubilant as we move forward into the so-called recent period. Because the

gush of colour is held back, it mobilizes more violence, potentializes the double energy: first the full encircling ring, the black line, incisive, definitive, then the flood of broad chromatic scales in a wash of colour. The colour then transforms the program, with a self-assurance all the more transgressive . . . for leaving the law of the trait intact in its inky light.

In a paper called 'Giotto's Joy' (1980), Julia Kristeva saw colour as, on the one hand, 'situated within the formal system of painting' (Kristeva, 1980: 216), and expressing the 'ideological values germane to a given culture' (*ibid.*: 219), but, on the other hand 'an instinctual pressure, an erotic implication of the subject' (*ibid.:* 220), and a 'physiologically supported drive' (*ibid.:* 219), which can 'destroy normativity' (*ibid.*: 221):

> Colour is the shattering of unity. Thus, it is through colour – colours – that the subject escapes its alienation within a code (representational, ideological, symbolic, and so forth) that it, as conscious subject accepts. Similarly it is through colour that western painting began to escape the constraints of narrative and perspective norms (as with Giotto) as well as representation itself (as with Cézanne, Matisse, Rothko, Mondrian).

What is the position of social semiotics in this debate? From linguistic theory it has inherited a somewhat Kantian schema, a schema separating 'content' and 'expression' (O'Halloran, 2008) in a way that leaves little doubt as to what is regarded as primary and what as secondary. Linguistic theory sees meaning as constructed at the abstract level of words and clauses (*content*) and then 'realized', made perceivable, either as speech or as writing (*expression*), but without this realization adding anything other than making it visible or audible, and hence communicable. Jakobson and Halle (1973: 152), for instance, said that speech sounds 'serve merely to differentiate, cement and partition or bring into relief the manifold meaningful units'. In Kress and van Leeuwen (2001: 4ff.), we followed this tradition in distinguishing an abstract 'design' stage at which content is given its communicable shape, and a concrete 'production' stage at which it is given its material, and hence perceivable expression. But we did also depart from it, in two ways. First we pointed out that the division between 'design' and 'production' is not inherent in all semiotic resources for all times. It is a way of thinking that stems from historically contingent semiotic practices, a historically specific division of labour between architects and builders, composers and performing musicians, playwrights and actors, etc., in which the design of the work is seen as its true creation and its performance or execution as a lesser creation which at best adds a degree of craftsmanship, taste or artistry. This division of labour began in the Renaissance, but it is not the only one possible. Jazz musicians, for instance, are composers as well as performers. And today 'performance' begins to be recognized again as a creation in its own right. Second, we pointed out that 'production' *does* add meaning. But we did not get very far in describing the kinds of meaning added by performance and the term 'add' still betrays the Kantian heritage. What kinds of meaning are produced in 'production'? Take speech, for example. Is the intonation of the living voice 'secondary', an enhancement of the primary meanings of the words, as has been argued for instance by Crystal (1975), or is it an independent strand of meaning, as has been argued for instance by Bolinger (1972)? And if so, what kind of meaning? Or think of music and theatre. Is the performance of a musical composition or a play an interpretation of the work of the composer or playwright, subservient to his or her ideas? Or can it be a creation in its own right? The problem is both are possible. The question has to be asked differently: What is, in a given place and time, and for a given semiotic practice, the dominant practice, and why? And: What kinds of theories and discourses exist to support this dominant practice?

In this context, colour is usually seen as 'expression' or 'production' rather than as 'content' or 'design' (e.g. O'Halloran, 2005, 2008; Kress and van Leeuwen, 2001; Painter, 2008). Although social semioticians do acknowledge that colour is expressive and meaningful, they do see its meanings as different from those that are expressed by language-like systems. O'Halloran (2008: 451) sees colour meaning as more 'multiple' and 'cross-functional' than the meanings expressed by linguistics systems, and this, she says, requires "a different approach to modeling and analyzing systems". Kress and van Leeuwen suggest that colour meanings come about through connotation and metaphor (2001: 72ff.), rather than through systematic grammatical systems, in a 'parametric' approach which will be discussed in more detail later in this book. Like O'Halloran and Kress and Van Leeuwen (2002), Painter, in a discussion of children's picture books (2008) recognizes the multi-functionality of colour, but then goes on to describe colour mainly in terms of 'mood' and 'ambience', using terms familiar from the psychologically oriented literature such as 'warm', 'vibrant', and 'active'. In writings of this kind, colour meaning is seen as different from linguistic meaning, and as a challenge to the linguistically inspired approach of social semiotics. But there is little dialogue with the affective, aesthetic and subversive aspects of colour which the poststructuralist philosophers have put on the agenda. One thing is clear. After a time in which colour has been restrained and repressed in favour of a more subdued and monochrome colour environment, and a more naturalistic approach to the use of colour in art, colour is now making a comeback as a medium of communication, gradually unfolding its wings, both in practice and in theory.

To sum up, colour has often been seen as secondary, as a matter of 'colouring in' already finished outline drawings. More recently, poststructuralist philosophers have reversed the hierarchy and contrasted form and colour in favour of colour, singing the praises of colour in near-erotic terms, or seeing it as subversive. This book is about the social uses of colour. But in contemporary culture, where the design industry, and the advertising and marketing industry, often seek to lend erotic appeal to social ideas and values and to the consumer goods that express them, the social and the individual, the normative and the erotic, are perhaps not as separate as the poststructuralists have made out.

1.3 Colour as communication

Not only philosophers such as Hegel, Barthes and Derrida, but also modern artists have, from the early twentieth century onwards, sung the praises of colour, heralding a reversal of the preference for *disegno* and *chiaroscuro*. Matisse, not unlike the poststructuralist philosophers, saw colour as 'a retinal sensation [that] destroys the calm of the surface and the contour' and as a 'tactile vitality comparable to the "vibrato" of the violin and voice' (quoted in Kristeva, 1980: 219). The Futurists saw it as subversive and, in a defiant manifesto, condemned 'faded, semidark and humiliating shades' and announced 'joyful' and 'exciting' colours in art and everyday life:

> Brown tints have never coursed beneath our skin. Yellow shines forth in our flesh, red blazes, green, blue and violet dance upon it with untold charms, voluptuous and caressing. How is it possible to still see the human face pink, now that our life, redoubled by noctambulism, has multiplied our perceptions as colourists? The human face is yellow, red, green, blue, violet. The pallor of a woman gazing in a jeweller's window is more

intensely iridescent than the prismatic fires of the jewels that fascinate her . . . The time has passed for our sensations in painting to be whispered. We wish them in future to sing and re-echo upon our canvases in deafening and triumphant flourishes.

(Umberto Boccioni, Carlo Carrà, Luigio Russolo, Giacomo Balla and Gino Severini, 'Futurist Painting: Technical Manifesto', 1910, quoted in Apollonio, 2009: 29)

Such 'defiant and triumphant' colours should also be introduced in everyday life, the Futurists said, for instance in dress:

Today we want to abolish: . . . all neutral, 'pretty', faded, fancy, semidark and humiliating shades . . . Futurist clothes shall therefore be . . . joyful. Clothes in exciting colours and iridescenses. Using muscular, ultra violet, ultra red, ultra turquoise, ultra green, bright yellows and vivid oranges, and rich vermillions. . . . If the Government does not drop its staid traditional dress of fear and indecisiveness, we will double, we will centuplicate the red of the tricolour which we wear.

(Giacomo Balla, 'Anti-neutral clothes manifesto',
Milan 1914, quoted in Koolhaas *et al.*, 2001: 308)

Simultaneously, a psychology of colour had emerged, from the late nineteenth century onwards. Like the later poststructuralist philosophers, these early psychologists saw colour as a highly immediate, individual feeling, and this idea influenced many of the artists who, in this period, sought to develop a non-representational, abstract art in which colour would have a direct effect, unmediated by representation. Experimental studies such as those of Stefănescu-Goangă established colour as 'a matter of the nerves', with direct psychological effects (see Gage, 1999: 192). Blue can calm, for instance, and red can excite. Such findings were soon applied to 'chromotherapy', colour healing, with commercial applications as in this 1918 advertisement (quoted in Gage, 1999: 208):

The sense of confinement from which [shell shock and nerve] patients suffer is done away with by painting the ceiling Firmament Blue, walls Sunlight Yellow, woodwork Spring Green and furniture Sunlight Primrose.

Gradually the world would become more colourful. The dreary regulation colours of public transport and the black of motor cars (Henry Ford for a long time produced only black cars) would be replaced by brighter colours, the grey suits of businessmen enlivened by colourful ties, the faded browns of domestic interiors modernized with brighter shades. Magazines, photographs, films, newspapers would, one by one, abandon black and white and move to colour. Even underwear, traditionally undyed, would acquire colour. But perhaps it is only in the last 20 years or so, in what I will call 'the new writing', and in relation to desktop publishing software, presentation software, and so on, that colour has made its most definite breakthrough, replacing the austerity of type-written and densely printed documents with a new emphasis on visuality, on layout, colour and typography. Business presentations and annual reports, invoices and forms, all are now produced in vivid colour, and the use of colour is available to anyone who has access to a computer.

As discussed in the previous section, French poststructuralist philosophers, just before the breakthrough of the computer, celebrated colour as 'blissful' and 'transgressive', and as subjective and individual, outside the reach of social conventions, rules and regulations. But today social rules and regulations are no longer separate from pleasure and 'bliss'.

Contemporary society enlists pleasure in the service of its rules and regulations. It seeks to combine learning and entertainment, work and pleasure, ideas and emotions. In the brochure shown in Figure 1.1, Xerox reports the outcome of a staff satisfaction questionnaire to its employees, using a diagram that combines the pie chart and the colour circle. The brochure contains two diagrams of this kind. One is headed 'Where we are now', the other 'Where we want to be'. Staff gave three kinds of feedback, the diagram suggests, bright, 'sunny' yellow feedback, shown on top ('Innovative – exciting – can do – yes and . . .'); pale blue feedback, shown bottom left ('Competitive . . . power – now – yes but . . .'); and pale lilac feedback, shown bottom right ('. . . If – maybe – caution – No but . . .'). As shown in Figure 1.1, 'yellow' staff members made comments such as 'I've got some good ideas for improvements', 'It's important to feel that you can influence things', 'We need to work together with management'. But this was still not quite what the company wanted them to say. The company wanted more emotion. It wanted words like 'great', 'exciting', 'enjoy'. It wanted a 'culture change' that would create people who 'solve problems, are dedicated to customer care and enjoy working for the organization'.

This is not too far away from the children's toys and books that teach children basic visual concepts, tied to generic words – and do so in vivid, sensual colour. A car might be visually defined by its basic form, a bubble with four wheels, and labelled, simply, 'car' – but all this is done in bright, primary colours. The conceptual combines with the aesthetic and sensory. Poststructuralist philosophers still kept mind and body separate, even as they celebrated the body. Modern society seeks to merge the two, socializing pleasure and making the social more pleasurable. Sigmund Freud was right in this respect. Pleasure does not exist in a vacuum. It is never separate from representation, always attached to mental representations of the world. A hedonistic society such as ours makes use of this to ensure the social cohesion and participation it needs to be able to function.

In this book I will try to show how colour and its pleasures are used for purposes of social communication, whether within smaller or larger social groups. As in earlier work, I will start out from Halliday's theory of the 'metafunctions' of communication (1978). According to Halliday, semiotic resources and their uses have developed to fulfil social needs. My example of the little black dress has already shown that this idea can be applied to the development of semiotic resources that draw specific colours into the sphere of social communication, such as black dyes. This emphasis on the social does not mean that I do not believe in individual colour preferences, or in the sensual attraction of colour. The very fact that our society recognizes individual colour preferences, and endows them with the authority of publicly funded research, means that, as a social semiotician, I cannot ignore them, and the sensual attraction of colour has been recognized throughout history, by those who celebrated it as well as by those who preached against it. But, unlike the early twentieth-century psychologists (and quite a few contemporary ones), I also know that other societies might not recognize this idea. The anthropologist Malinowski (1935: 50), during his fieldwork in the Trobriand Islands, saw children pick up attractive flowers or colourful leaves, only to be told by adults 'It has no name. It is just a weed' or 'Throw it away, since it is a weed'. The Trobriand islanders clearly did not value individual colour preferences, and could not conceive of something being beautiful without having a social function.

According to Halliday, three principal 'metafunctions' are simultaneously present in every act of social communication, the *ideational function*, the function of constructing representations of the world; the *interpersonal function*, the function of enacting (or helping to enact) communicative interactions characterized by specific social purposes and specific social relations; and the *textual function*, the function of marshalling communicative acts into larger wholes, into the communicative events or texts that realize specific social practices such as conversations, lectures, reports, etc. In an earlier publication (Kress and van Leeuwen, 2002), we tried to show that colour, today, *can* fulfil all three of these functions.[1] Ideationally, it can be used to denote specific people, places and things as well as classes of people, places and things and more general ideas. The colours of flags, for instance, denote specific nations, and modern corporations increasingly use specific colours or colour schemes to denote their unique identities. Car manufacturers legally protect the differences between the 'Reflex Silver' of the VW, which has a slight, warming yellowish cast, the pinkiness of Audi's 'Silver Metallic', the lightness of Suzuki's 'Silky Silver' and the silvery silveriness of Mercedes' 'Brilliant Silver' (*Observer Magazine*, 3 November 2002), so that others will not be able to use them. Universities also use colour to signal their identities. The Open University, for instance, stipulates:

> Two colours . . . for formal applications such as high-quality stationery and degree certificates – blue (reference PMS 300) for the shield and lettering and yellow (PMS 123) for the circular inset. Single colour stationery should be on blue (PMS 300) if possible.
>
> (Goodman and Graddol, 1996: 119)

On maps, colours can denote water, arable land, deserts and so on, on uniforms rank, as already in medieval heraldry. In the safety code designed by colour theorist Faber Birren (Lacy, 1996: 75) green identifies first-aid equipment, red identifies hoses and valves. In the London Underground green identifies the District Line and red the Central Line. More abstract ideas, too, have been expressed by colour for a long time. In medieval colour symbolism black stood for penance, white for innocence and purity, and red for the Pentecostal fire, for instance. In the flag of the ANC in South Africa, green stands for the land, gold for its wealth and black for the African people (Archer, in press).

Colour is also used to convey 'interpersonal' meaning. Just as language allows us to realize speech acts, so colour allows us to realize 'colour acts'. It can be and is used to *do* things to or for each other – to intimidate through 'power dressing', to warn against obstructions and other hazards by painting them orange, or even to subdue people: 'Pink, properly applied, relaxes hostile and aggressive individuals within 15 minutes' (Lacy, 1996: 89). According to *The Guardian*'s *Office Hours Supplement*:

> Colours are very powerful and can reduce or raise stress levels, believes Lilian Verner-Bonds, author of *Colour Healing*. Bright reds are energizing and are good for offices in the banking or entertainment fields. Green is useful if there is discord or disharmony as it is soothing. Blue is rated as the best colour for gently encouraging activity.
>
> (*The Guardian*, 3 September 2001: 5)

According to the same article, adding colour to documents can increase readers' attention span by more than 80 per cent and 'an invoice that has the amount of money in colour is 30% more likely to be paid on time than a mono-colour one'. In all these cases, it is not colour itself doings these things, it is people doing these things *with* colour, using colour to interact, albeit in a rather manipulative way, to energize or calm down – or to express the values that go with such activities, to say, as it were: 'I am exciting' or 'I am calm'.

Finally colour can be used 'textually', to create coherence between the different elements of a larger whole and/or to distinguish between its different parts. In many buildings the different colours of doors, floor coverings or other features distinguish different departments from each other, while at the same time creating unity and coherence within each of these departments, and colour can create this kind of coherence also in texts. In *Pasos*, a Spanish language textbook (Martín and Ellis, 2001), the chapter headings and page numbers of each chapter have a distinct colour, the section headings are red, and the 'activities' (e.g. 'Make phrases with *es* or *está*') have a purple heading and number. Many books on website design recommend using colour to give sites a unified identity.

There are two further points to be made here. First, colour fulfils these three metafunctions *simultaneously*. The colours on a map might have an ideational function, but they also and at the same time retain their interpersonal value, their appealing brightness or stuffy dullness, and they also help create textual cohesion and unity. Again, contemporary scientific visualizations might be thought of as primarily ideational, creating a clear distinction between different elements, say in brain tomography. But they are often as aesthetically appealing as abstract paintings and would not go amiss in a frame in a lounge-room.

To sum up, in the twentieth century, after a rather 'monochrome' period, colour began to extend its semiotic reach. Heralded by artists and thinkers, it soon began to play a more important role in the everyday expression of ideational, interpersonal and textual meanings, while all the time retaining its sensual attraction, so investing social communication with pleasure and sensuality. It is this new role of colour that I will try to elucidate in this book, after first setting the context by discussing the historical development of colour meanings and colour theories, and the issue of colour naming.

Exercises

1   Judging by the following extract from an article by Paul Overy (Koolhaas *et al*., 2001: 122–3), how would you describe the famous architect Norman Foster's position in the 'design versus colour' debate, and which of the 'metafunctions' do you think he acknowledges in his use of colour?

> Norman Foster recently made a series of colour sketches for a light aircraft, a Robin Regent. Initially he thought of painting the fuselage a rich, deep blue – a colour he has used for exterior and interior accents in some of his recent buildings. He explored a combination of the blue with yellow trim to emphasize the lines of the wing and fuselage, and also considered unifying the form of the canopy by painting the struts and roof dark grey to blend in with the acrylic panels. But in the end, he decided to paint the entire plane white because he came to the conclusion that the form of this classic aircraft did not need the distraction of any cosmetic embellishment. For an aircraft which would be used mostly in the summer, Foster argued that white was also the best colour to reduce solar gain – hence the decision to reject the idea of dark grey for the canopy. Other colours were confined to details, such as the propeller spinner highlighted in red because it marked a potential hazard on the ground and would be more conspicuous in the air. Colour was also used to denote the area at the wing root which was reinforced and could be walked upon – as opposed to the more fragile covering elsewhere. Finally he added the blue symbol of the EC flag to the fin.

> The Robin is a very popular light aircraft in France, where it is immediately recognizable, partly because of its shape, but also because it is invariably painted in a standard factory colour scheme. Foster's treatment of the aircraft, however, transformed its appearance so completely that apparently even traffic controllers did not recognize it. On seeing the plane from the control tower they would immediately ask: 'What type of

aircraft is that?' Foster explains that the greatest difference between the normal Robin and his own was that he used a single colour to unite the intrinsic form of the aircraft – to emphasize the purity of its aerodynamic shape. Other colours were then employed as signals to convey information. (He talks at some length about how colour is used in nature either to attract attention or to camouflage.) Foster's thinking about colour in relation to his personal light aircraft is revealing and can be extended to explain the philosophy about the use of colour in his buildings. Although there are some exceptions, he tends to emphasize spaces, both inside and out, by the use of a single neutral or metallic colour, working with limited accents of other colours to create 'signals'.

2 Identify a community in which a particular colour is preferred or prescribed as the only or dominant colour for dress. Research what reasons are given for the choice of this colour, either in prescriptive texts and/or in one or more interviews you might want to conduct with members of the community.

3 Design a colour scheme for the review section of the weekly magazine of a major newspaper. It should distinguish between book reviews, film reviews, theatre reviews, music reviews and art reviews, but provide some overall coherence as well. Explain your choice of colours.

2 Colour Meanings

2.1 The many meanings of colour

The same colour can express many different meanings and the same meaning can be expressed by many different colours. In India and China brides wear red, in Europe and North America white. In the Middle Ages, red was the colour of princes as well as of executioners and prostitutes (Pastoureau, 2008: 99), and black signified simplicity and penitence as well as sorrow, death and sin. In one and the same society or period, different, contradictory systems can exist alongside each other, each covering one small domain of meaning. In the Middle Ages, green could mean 'hope' in the context of the triad 'faith' (white), 'hope' (green) and 'charity' (red), and 'justice' in the context of the triad 'temperance' (blue), 'justice' (green) and 'fortitude' (diamond[1]). It is not so different today. In the bathroom the hot water tap is red, on a traffic light red tells you to stop. In American university gowns red is the colour of theology, in politics it is the colour of socialism, communism and revolution. In Dutch supermarkets, blue is the colour of decaf (there are red, gold and blue coffees), as well as the colour of milk (there are green dairy products (yoghurt), blue dairy products (milk) and red dairy products (churned milk).

Despite the title of this book, and despite the efforts of psychologists to construct universal psychological meanings for colour, there does not seem to be a single 'language of colour'. Instead there is a multitude of codes, conventional associations and uses of colour, many of them with limited contexts of application and limited semantic domains. As Pastoureau has said (2001: 8):

> Colour is a complex cultural construct that resists generalization, and, indeed analysis itself . . . Many authors search for the universal or archetypal truths they imagine reside in colour, but colour is first and foremost a social phenomenon, There is no transcultural truth to colour perception.

Nevertheless, there have been, and still are, broader trends and tendencies – colour systems related to religions or empires, such as those in India and China – or the global system that underlies today's use of colour in the creation of lifestyle and corporate identities, and in the new, multimodal forms of writing that integrate language with visual resources such as layout, typography and colour. It is this new, global approach to the communicative use of colour I will explore in this book, starting from Chapter 5. But before doing so, we need to understand the tradition it grew out of, starting, in this chapter, with three key approaches to the meaning of colour in Western history – *colour symbolism*, *colour naturalism*, and *colour as affect and effect*. These three approaches originated in this order, and for this reason this chapter is written as a history. But all three continue to exist, and all three continue to play an important role in the contemporary 'language of colour'.

2.2 Colour symbolism

In the Middle Ages, colour was used for the *symbolic expression of ideas and values* – sacred, religious ideas and values as well as secular, chivalrous ones. The colour of dress played an important role in the expression of religious ideas. In the sixth century, St Benedictus, founder of the Benedictine order, had told his monks to use simple undyed wool, which they should spin and weave themselves ('Let the monks not be concerned about the colour nor the thickness of these things [i.e. items of clothing]' (quoted in Pastoureau, 2009: 40) but from the ninth century on, Benedictine monks began to wear black, which was understood to be the colour of humility and penitence, and of poverty and simplicity (as pure black dyes did not yet exist at the time, the fabric was in reality probably dark grey or dark brown). At the same time, another monastic order, the Cistercians, began to wear white, which was understood to be the colour of innocence, purity and eternal life, and this resulted in a debate about the meaning of colour that would last more than two decades. In 1124, Peter the Venerable, the Benedictine abbot of Cluny wrote a letter to Bernard, the Cistercian abbot of Clairvaux, accusing him of vanity and pride for displaying the colour of glory and resurrection, rather than the colour of humility and renouncement which he thought befitted monks who had turned their back on the world. Bernard responded that black was the colour 'of death and sin', whereas white was the colour of 'purity, innocence and all the virtues' (see Pastoureau, 2008: 66). Other orders, too, prescribed their own colour, to signify their distinct values and beliefs.

'Liturgical' colours, with symbolic meanings appropriate to the different periods of the religious calendar, were also important, and used, among other things, for the dress of priests in these different periods. Initially different regions did this in different ways, but around the year 1200 Pope Innocent III ordered greater homogeneity. White should be used on the feasts of the Virgin, and on Christmas and Easter, he decreed, as it is the colour of innocence and purity. Black should be used for Advent and Lent, as well as for Masses for the deceased, as it is the colour of penance and mourning. Red should be used for the feasts of the Apostles and Martyrs, and for Pentecost, as it reminds of the blood of Christ and the Pentecostal fire. Green, which Innocent III regarded as 'halfway between white, black and red' (Pastoureau, 2001: 40) should be used on all other days. Innocent's contemporary Siccardus of Cremona disagreed, arguing that red vestments and hangings signified charity. In due course such debates on the meaning of colour would become more intricate and learned, so that Popes needed their Masters of Ceremony to act as colour advisers, as in the case of Pope Alexander VI who wanted to dress in white when leading prayers for the victims of a flood, but was advised to wear violet instead, because white would express happiness and rejoicing, while violet would express mourning (Gage, 1999: 84).

The art of the Middle Ages used colour to identify biblical characters and Saints. The Virgin Mary wore a blue robe, St Peter a blue tunic and a yellow cloak, for instance. Identifying colours of this kind were chosen for their symbolic appropriateness, and as theological interpretations changed, so did the colours. The Virgin Mary, for instance, had first worn dark clothes, to express grief, but later she wore blue, the colour of sanctity and divinity, and still later, after the Church had adopted the doctrine of the immaculate conception, in the mid-nineteenth century, she wore white, the colour of purity and virginity (Pastoureau, 2001: 49ff.). Colour references to religious ideas were apparently well understood by the public of the time (Gage 1999: 84). In a fresco in the Palazzo Pubblica in Siena, for example, Ambrogio Lorenzetti used blue to express Temperance, green to express Justice, diamond to express Fortitude, and carbuncle (a fiery red) to express Prudence. In another painting he labelled Faith, Hope and Charity by means of words as well as by the colours white, green and red.

Heraldic colour came into use because the medieval knights, rendered anonymous by their armour, had to be recognizable from a distance. For this reason they painted their shields in bright colours, with distinct, individual patterns which eventually became hereditary. Over time, heraldry developed its own set of colours or 'tinctures' – 'or' (gold or yellow), 'argent' (silver), 'gules' (red), 'azure' (blue), 'sable' (black) and 'vert' (green) – and its own meanings. The thirteenth-century Icelandic *Didrecks Saga*, for instance, explains that Heine the Proud carried a blue shield to signify his cold breast and grim heart, while Fasold and his brother Ecke had red shields to signify their love of fighting, and Hornbogi of Wendland and his son Amelung brown shields to express worth and courtesy. A mid-thirteenth-century French poem, *Ordene de Chevalerie*, describes how a knight, at his investiture, was dressed in a white robe to show his cleanliness, a scarlet cloak 'to remind him of his duty to shed blood for the Church', brown stockings 'to remind him of the earth in which he will eventually lie', and a white girdle, to signify chastity (Gage, 1999: 84). In Arthurian literature, the hero's path is often blocked by the sudden appearance of a knight in plain arms, who therefore cannot be identified. Red Knights tend to have evil intentions, Black Knights are important persons who, for one reason or another, hide their identity, while White Knights (as is still remembered today) are good knights who will protect the hero, and Green Knights overconfident young knights who create disorder and chaos (Pastoureau, 2009: 59). A modern summary of the meanings of heraldic colour has red expressing 'courage and zeal', blue 'piety and sincerity', yellow/gold 'honour and loyalty', green 'growth and hope', white/silver 'faith and purity', and black 'grief and penitence' (Birren, 1961: 173). In short, the Knight's code was 'an identity badge which defined his position within the socio-ethical code of chivalry and provided the means of public accountability for his behaviour' (Huxtable, 2006: 211). Eventually not only knights, but also magistrates, merchants and rich artisans acquired arms (Pastoureau, 2004: 15), at least in continental Europe, and the tradition continues today in the arms of companies (e.g. the lions and eagles on the bonnet emblems of motor cars) and corporate bodies (e.g. cities), and in flags (which generally use traditional heraldic colours), banners, sports shirts, and logos.

The relation between the signifier and the signified – in our case, between colour and its meaning – has long been a key issue in semiotics. How did medieval writers explain this relation, and how different was their reasoning from ours, today? Early writings on colour were personal reflections that did not necessarily document common practices of inter-pretation, but gradually colour began to be discussed more systematically, and writers began to agree on at least certain meanings, such as white for purity and innocence, black for abstinence, penance and suffering, and red for passion, martyrdom, sacrifice and divine love. There was less agreement on the other colours. Red, white and black seem to have been the most fundamental and most 'regulated' colours. To defend their arguments, many writers cited classical authorities such as Aristotle as well as more recent authors. The late fourteenth-century English heraldic writer Johannes de Bado Aureo based himself on his teacher, Master Francis, who had divided the colours into three groups, primary colours (white and black), secondary colours (blue, yellow and red), and tertiary colours, quite a different classification from the one we use today. Writing on heraldry, he was concerned with the status and ranking of colours and argued that, though others had ranked black rather low (and gold and red high), they would have to be wrong, because the master has said that black is a primary colour (see Gage, 1999: 89). Strengthening an argument by invoking authorities is, of course, still common today, for instance in art and design textbooks which often quote the colour meanings suggested by key twentieth-century artists such as Kandinsky and Mondrian.

Other arguments were based on everyday observation. While Bartolo de Sasferrato, a fourteenth-century Italian jurist, had mixed empirical and logical reasoning, arguing that white is noble because it represents light, and black therefore logically *least* noble, as it is the opposite of white, Lorenzo Valla asked why white should be more noble than other colours, because, he said, surely people prefer red or purple silk over white linen. And why should black be ranked so low, he also asked, if it is the colour of the centre of our eyes? (Gage, 1999: 89).

Other arguments were based on analogies with objects of the same colour. Meanings associated with these objects could then be transferred to their colour. Analogies with the four elements and with gemstones had been used since antiquity. Sometimes this had led to complex systems of correspondences, in which colours were related, not just to gemstones and their moral qualities, but also to metals, humours, elements, planets, signs of the Zodiac and days of the week. In an anonymous French treatise of the late fourteenth century, blue connoted sapphire as well as praise, beauty, the sanguine temperament, the planet Venus, Gemini, Libra and Aquarius, air, fine silver and Friday (*ibid.*: 83). Such arguments, too, are still used today, for instance by the linguist Wierzbicka (1996: 315) who argued that yellow is universally seen as 'warm' because it is the colour of the sun, or in a textbook on colour for artists and designers (Feisner, 2006: 122ff.) which derives colour meanings from associations with nature (e.g. yellow signifies 'caution' by reference to the yellow and black markings on insects which warn predators to keep their distance), and from associations with cultural objects (e.g. red signifies compassion by reference to the Red Cross).

By the early sixteenth century, colour had become a key theme for scholarly debate. Books by Lorenzo Valla and Fulvio Pellegrini Morato ran into many editions and were read until well into the nineteenth century. But another way of thinking about colour was to overtake it – the scientific way. Debates about colour symbolism began to be seen as scholastic hair-splitting. Mario Equicola, writing in 1525, pointed at the incompatibility of the accounts of colour meaning of his time and advocated using colour for 'variety' rather than for symbolic meaning: colours with identical chemical constitution should not be placed next to each other (Gage, 1993: 120). Morato agreed – choosing colours for their meaning might result in aesthetically unsatisfactory art.

Nevertheless, colour symbolism continued to exist, for instance in flags. In the American flag, as stipulated by the Great Seal of 1782, white signified purity and innocence, red hardiness and valour, and blue vigilance, perseverance and justice (Feisner, 2006: 129). Modern flags, too, refer to traditional symbolic values, and are even experiencing a resurgence, as they are now no longer only associated with nation states, but also with nationless peoples, sports clubs and so on. The flag of the United Democratic Front in South Africa, launched in 1982, had black for the African people, yellow or gold for the country's wealth, and red to signify the movement's alignment with leftist politics. The ANC dropped the red, and replaced it with green, for the land. During apartheid, people possessing items bearing these colours risked being beaten up, arrested, or even killed (Archer, in press). From the late nineteenth century on, symbolism began to be taken up in art again. For Franz von Stück, a German symbolist painter, red signified 'passion', yellow 'danger', green 'hope', and blue 'mystery, intellectuality and poetic worth' (Gage, 1999: 191). Malevich, in his abstract paintings, used a schema in which black meant 'economy', red 'revolution', and white 'action'. More recently colour symbolism has become important in lifestyle identity and corporate branding, as I will discuss in more detail in Chapter 7. The website of Progyms, a health products company, explains that violet symbolizes the ultimate force on earth while beige signifies serenity: 'The harmonious combination of the two colours reflects the innate power and purity of natural resources . . . PROGYMS aims to be a synergy of strength and serenity.'

Social semiotics (Kress and Van Leeuwen, 2006: 105–6) defines symbolism as the relation between a *carrier* (e.g. a medieval Knight) and a *symbolic attribute* (e.g. the colour of his arms) in which the attribute establishes the meaning or identity of the carrier. The attribute must have one or more of the following characteristics (cf. Hermeren, 1969):

- It is made conspicuous, by being placed in the foreground, exaggerated in size, specially well lit, represented in specially fine detail or sharp focus – or by means of conspicuous colour or tone.

- It is somehow unnatural or unrealistic (in the case of a picture) or without practical function (in the case of the whole, or a part of, an object, an item of clothing, a building, etc.).

- It is pointed at, or held, in a way that has no function other than displaying the attribute to the viewer.

- It is conventionally associated with symbolic values.

In medieval painting the Christ Child, standing on the lap of the Virgin Mary, might hold an apple which is not only disproportionately large, but also held in a way that makes it clear he is not about to eat it. The aim is to draw the viewer's attention to the fact that it is a symbol of the 'original sin' which Christ has atoned for, the eating of the forbidden fruit in the Garden of Eden. In the age of naturalism, such symbols do not yet disappear, but they are no longer depicted unnaturalistically. In Jan Van Eyck's 'St Jerome in his study', there is an apple on a shelf, behind the brooding Saint. It is neither extra large, nor particularly conspicuous. Panofsky (1971) has called such symbols 'disguised symbols' – the apple can either be interpreted as just happening to lie on that shelf, forgotten by the Saint, and realistically depicted, as it would have been in a photograph, or as a symbol and as the issue the Saint is meditating about in his study. Modern media images use both open and disguised symbolism. Much of the symbolism in feature films, for instance, is disguised and does not draw attention to itself. But advertisements and fashion photos contain a great deal of open symbolism. The models in fashion photos often hold objects in stylized, unnatural ways that show they are meant to be understood as symbolic attributes rather than objects for use – a spanner signifies toughness, spectacles dangling from the model's fingers, thoughtfulness, and so on. Even everyday newspaper photos of people-in-the-news can have symbolic attributes. Often they are 'grab and grins', as the photographers say, pictures in which people hold objects that index their identity – for instance a filmmaker is photographed with a can of film in her hands, a writer of grisly horror stories with a black cat on his lap.

2.3 Colour naturalism

In the Middle Ages people loved strong, intense colours, in life as well as in art. Those who could afford it dressed in bright colours, as illustrated by this twelfth-century quote from Chrétien de Troyes (Eco, 2002: 106):

The lining was of white ermine, the finest and most beautiful you could see. The purple robe was cunningly worked with little crosses in various colours, violet and vermilion and turquoise, white and green, violet and yellow.

Paintings and illustrators used brilliant primary colours, as prescribed by the writer of an anonymous fourteenth-century book (quoted in Eco, 2002: 108):

> There are eight colours most naturally necessary for illumination, namely black, white, red, yellow, light blue, violet, pink and green. Some of these are natural, others artificial.

But from about the mid-fifteenth century, Europe entered a black-and-white age that would last until at least the end of the nineteenth century (with a short intermezzo in the age of Enlightenment, from about 1720 to 1780, when especially pastel colours were in vogue). Artists began to favour *chiaroscuro*, the play of light and dark, over colour. State officials, university professors, and merchants and bankers began to wear black, and while medieval manuscripts had been bright and colourful, the printed word and the engraved image introduced a monochrome world of meaning. In Northern European Protestant churches, stained glass windows were replaced with clear glass, murals were white-washed, and paintings, statues and colourful liturgical vestments removed, as can be seen in Dutch church interior paintings of the time. As Calvin had declared, the most beautiful ornament in a church is the word of God.

The last vestiges of this black-and-white world are still with us. Most people still wear black, dark blue or grey clothes to work, and black still 'conveys elegance, sophistication and a touch of mystery', in the words of fashion designer Ana Sekularac (quoted in Mora, 2009: 169). Although Hollywood movies are now increasingly 'colourized', black and white can still be a mark of artistic distinction in the 'art house' cinema, and the art of cinematography continues to be an art of lighting, taking its cues from Rembrandt and Caravaggio, and keeping colour subdued, although things are different in animation movies which were the first to acquire colour, in 1932.

In the art of this monochrome world, colour not only became 'secondary', an embellishment, it also lost its semiotic role, as it now began to be used, not for its symbolic value, but naturalistically, to depict the world as it appears to the eye. What mattered now was not what colour meant, but how it could help artists create an illusion of reality. The theoretical literature stopped debating colour symbolism and started focusing on meteorological, physical and optical issues – the sun, clouds, raindrops, and especially the phenomena of reflection and refraction of light. Alberti, whose treatise *On Painting* (1435) introduced the theory and practice of perspective, recommended that painters 'learn from nature and from objects themselves' (Gage, 1993: 118) so as to better understand the way surfaces 'receive' light. And Leonardo da Vinci began to look at the world in the new spirit of science, trying to translate his observations into painting experiments and techniques, as can be seen in this quote from 1506 (da Vinci, 2005: 97) which records his observations (e.g. of the colour of distant mountains) and scientific experiments ('admitting sunbeams through holes into a dark chamber') as well as his painting experiments ('lay a thin and transparent coating of white over an intense black'):

> The atmosphere assumes this azure hue by reason of the particles of moisture which catch the rays of the sun. Again, we may note the difference in particles of dust, or particles of smoke, in the sunbeams admitted through holes into a dark chamber, when the former will look ashy grey and the thin smoke will appear of the most beautiful blue. It may be seen again in the dark shadows of distant mountains when the air between the eye and those shadows will look very blue, though the brightest parts of those mountains will not differ much from their true colours. But if anyone wishes for a final proof let him

paint a board with various colours, among them an intense black; and over all let him lay a very thin and transparent [coating of] white. He will then see that this transparent white will nowhere show a more beautiful blue than over the black, but it must be very thin and finely ground.

He also argued for an infinite number of degrees of shadow rather than the traditional four degrees, because, he said, 'shadow is a more powerful agent than light, for it can impede and entirely deprive bodies of their light, while light can never entirely expel shadows from a body' (*ibid*.: 76). And he observed the effects of colour in reflections and shadows, almost anticipating Impressionism. 'Every object is more or less tinged by the colour [of the object] placed opposite'; 'A shadow is always affected by the colour of the surface on which it is cast'; and 'The surface of every opaque body is affected by the [reflected] colour of the objects surrounding it' (*ibid.*: 98).

The naturalistic art of the seventeenth-century Dutch masters had theological approval. According to Calvin, art should celebrate creation. Painters should use moderation, seek harmony of form, and represent what they saw. The most beautiful colours, Calvin had written, are those of nature. Hence these painters' focus on portraits, still-lives and land-scapes, and their restrained, at times almost black and white, palette (see Pastoureau, 2008: 125) – according to Van Gogh, Frans Hals had 27 blacks on his palette (Gage, 1993: 159).

Isaac Newton's discovery of the colour spectrum would officially abolish black and white as colours, and establish the opposition between 'black and white' and 'colour' that is still with us. Until then, people had always regarded black and white as colours and arranged colours on a linear scale, generally with white (maximum light) on one side, black (maximum dark) on the other, red in the middle, and the other colours in between. In a 1672 presentation to the Royal Society, Newton presented colour as a circle, without white and black, and showed that white light is a combination of all the colours of light in the right proportions. Initially he had segmented the colours of the rainbow in five distinct colours (red, yellow, green, blue and purple), but in his 1672 address he added orange and indigo. From this time on, black and white were no longer regarded as colours, or rather, colour was separated off from the dominant medium of black-and-white and given a secondary place. At the same time, red was displaced from the centre and banished to the margins of the spectrum. Most importantly, colour was now no longer part of the monochrome world of meaning. Just as phonetics treats the sounds of speech without reference to language as a meaning-making system, using its own physiological and physical methods, so colour was now split into two disciplines that did not sit easily with each other – on the one hand chemistry and physics, and later the physiology of colour perception, sciences which looked at colour as an objective phenomenon, separate from the subjective, human world; on the other hand the emerging psychology of colour, which gave a central place to human subjectivity. Early scientists had still seen colour as subjective and impervious to scientific method. Newton now demonstrated that it could be measured and controlled, something that would turn out to be decisive for the development of colour printing and colour film. As Gage has said (1993: 152):

Colorimetry would invade practice and theory. In many areas chromatic scales, schemas and sample charts were developed to demonstrate the standards and rules colour had to obey.

This development has continued to our day. Important uses of colour, for instance in film and photography, and also in computer games, are still judged by naturalistic criteria of verisimilitude such as flesh tones, rather than on the basis of what colour communicates, and radical experiments with colour remain rare in these media.

In social semiotics (Van Leeuwen, 2005: 160ff.; Kress and Van Leeuwen, 2006: 154ff.), naturalism is defined in terms of *modality*, and modality, in turn, is defined as referring to semiotic resources that express how true or how real a given representation should be taken to be. Language, for example, has modal auxiliaries such as 'might', 'will' and 'must', which express degrees of probability. When you say 'it might rain', you mean this to be taken as less probable than 'it will rain'. And language has other modality devices, other kinds of modality, as well. It can for instance realize 'objective modality', through phrases like 'It is probable that', or 'It is more than likely that', as well as 'subjective modality', through the use of 'mental process verbs' such as 'guess', 'believe', and 'know'. It is important to note that high modality does not guarantee actual high truth value. High modality can be used to lend apparent credibility to something which is, in fact, not true, and vice versa. A fairytale can be told with great realism, and it is equally possible to use low modality to cast doubt on something that actually exists or has existed – think of the Holocaust deniers. In visual communication, modality can use *naturalistic*, *abstract*, or *sensory* truth criteria. In the case of naturalistic modality, the truth criterion is perceptual. It rests on the idea that the more a visual representation resembles what we would see if we saw the represented things in reality, the truer people will think it is. The means of representation which the Renaissance artists began to develop and which culminated in photography (perspective, detailed representation of the play of light and shade, detailed modulation of colour, and so on) were all developed in the service of this kind of truth. But there are other visual truths. In abstract modality, the truth criterion is cognitive, based on whether a representation represents a general pattern underlying superficially different instances, or the deeper 'essence' of what is represented. Here the use of naturalistic representation devices is reduced. Illustrations in science textbooks may be simple, two-dimensional line drawings, for instance, and yet they are to be taken as representing scientific truths. In sensory modality, finally, the truth criterion is emotive, based on the effect of pleasure or displeasure created by visual representations. This is conveyed by 'excess', by going beyond the constraints of naturalistic representation, by using extra deep perspective, for instance, and of course, extra vivid colour rather than the subdued colours of naturalistic representation. For the moment it is important to note that, from the Renaissance on, naturalistic modality became the dominant truth criterion in visual representation. And to some degree, it still is, even in new media such as computer games.

2.4 Colour as affect and effect

In the course of the nineteenth century, a new approach to the meaning of colour emerged, to a large degree stimulated by Johann Wolfgang von Goethe's remarkable book *Theory of Colours* (1970 [1810]). In most of this book Goethe argues with Newton and develops his own theory of colour, based on the opposition between dark and light, recognizing only yellow and blue as true, pure colours (yellow on the side of brightness, blue on the side of darkness) and seeing red as produced from yellow and blue by a process of *Steigerung* ('augmentation'). But it is not because of this now outdated theory that Goethe's book is so important. It is because, unlike Newton, Goethe *did* talk about the subjective, human aspects of colour, presenting ideas about the meaning of colour that would profoundly influence how we talk about colour today. It was Goethe who first formulated the idea that colour is primarily affective (colour, he said, 'is immediately associated with the emotions of the mind', (*ibid*.:

304)); the idea that colour can express 'character'; the idea that people have innate colour preferences; and the idea that colour can have direct, unmediated effects on people.

'In dress', said Goethe, 'we associate the character of the colour with the character of the person' (*ibid.*: 326). Yellow is 'bright, serene, gay, softly exciting' (*ibid.*: 307) while blue brings 'cold, shade, gloom, melancholy'. Here, colour meanings (Goethe called them 'moral associations', *ibid.*: 304) no longer denoted theological virtues such as 'humility' and 'penitence', or chivalrous virtues such as 'honour', 'loyalty' and 'bravery', but the modern narcissistic 'personality traits' that would come to dominate the discourses of contemporary popular psychology and its applications. Anticipating modern interior design colour consultants, Goethe even suggested that yellow 'in dress, hangings, carpeting, etc.' has 'a magnificent and noble effect' and that 'rooms that are hung with pure blue appear in some degree larger, but at the same time empty and cold' (*ibid.*: 311).

As for colour preferences, 'primitives', children and people from Southern countries, Goethe said, prefer bright colours (*ibid.*: 310), and women have stronger colour preferences than men (*ibid.*: 328):

> The female sex in youth is attached to rose colour and sea-green, in age to violet and dark green. The fair-haired prefer violet as opposed to light yellow, the brunettes blue as opposed to yellow-red.

Finally, colour has direct sensory effects: 'Experience teaches us that particular colours excite particular states of feeling' (*ibid.*: 305). Blue, for example (*ibid.*: 312) has a 'somewhat active character'. 'Its exciting power', however, is 'of a very different kind from that of red-yellow. It may be said to disturb rather than enliven'. Goethe even foreshadowed 'chromotherapy': 'The healing powers ascribed to gems, may have arisen from this indefinable pleasure [i.e. pleasure in the display of colour]' (*ibid.*: 305). The effect is greatest when the patient is 'in a room of one colour, or looks through a coloured glass' to 'attune the eye and the mind in mere unison with itself' (*ibid.*: 306).

Here, Goethe made a semiotically important distinction, the distinction between the *effect* of colour and the symbolic *meaning* of colour. Some symbolic meanings, he said, can be directly understood, because they 'coincide with nature', others are 'allegorical' and can only be understood if they are first communicated in words (*ibid.*: 350):

> An application [of colour] coinciding with nature may be called symbolical, since the colour would be employed in conformity with its effect, and would at once express its meaning, e.g., pure red to designate majesty. Another application is nearly allied to this, it might be called allegorical. In this there is more of an accident and caprice, inasmuch as the meaning of the sign must first be communicated to us before we know what it is to signify, e.g. green for hope.

Because of its emotive effect, Goethe argued, colour is an important resource for artists. This idea would soon be picked up by Romantic painters. The German '*Lucasbund*' painters Friedrich Overbeck and Franz Pforr devised their own colour codes for expressing character, but only in women, because they thought that the colour of male dress was determined by their profession (Gage, 1999: 188–90). According to these painters, black hair goes with black and violet, black and blue, white and violet, and these colours signify a 'proud and cool', yet 'cheerful and happy' personality. Blonde hair goes with blue and grey or grey and crimson, and signifies 'solitariness, modesty, goodheartedness and calm', while blonde hair with grey and crimson is expressive of 'feminine amiability, or rather, true femininity'. Reddish brown goes with crimson cast, violet-grey and black and signifies 'happiness and good temper, innocent roguishness, naiveté and cheerfulness' (*ibid.*). The Expressionists, would revive affective colour meanings of this kind, using colour in non-naturalistic ways, as a 'stimulus', a 'non-associative psychological effect', also for subjects other than dress – contemporary critics would attack their 'green skies', 'violet meadows' and 'yellow streams' (Gage, 1993: 207).

By the end of the nineteenth century Goethe's ideas would find their way into a new science – the science of psychology. Although late nineteenth-century colour psychology mostly occupied itself with the physiology of colour perception, there was also research on the affective meanings and effects of colour, and on synaesthesia, starting especially in Leipzig, where, in the 1890s, Wilhelm Wundt had established the first laboratory for conducting psychological experiments. Wundt's own experiments were directly influenced by Goethe, taking the primary polarity of yellow and blue as their point of departure and finding that these colours do create the 'active' versus 'passive' sensations Goethe had discussed in 1812 (Gage, 1999: 252). Jonas Cohn, one of his co-workers, discovered that young men like highly saturated colours and contrasting colours and concluded that humans have a natural propensity for strong colours which may then be repressed by society. Somewhat later, Wundt's student Florian Stefănescu-Goangă conducted a series of experiments to study the emotions colour produces, finding, for instance, that blue is 'calming, depressing, peaceful, quiet, serious, nostalgic, melancholic, cool, calm and dreamy' (Gage, 1999: 192). In France, Charles Féré had followed up on another tip from Goethe, placing subjects in a room and exposing them to coloured light. He found that red stimulates, while violet calms down, just as did 'Italian mad doctors', according to an 1883 overview by the psychologist F. Galton (*ibid.*):

> There is no doubt that blue has a calming effect and red an irritating one, for the Italian mad doctors find an advantage in putting their irritable patients in a room lighted with blue light and their apathetic ones under red light.

In 1940, the Swiss psychologist Max Lüschler started using colour in personality testing. His subjects had to put eight colours in order of preference. Blue, the most often preferred colour, signified 'concentric, passive, perceptive, unifying', hence also 'tranquility, tenderness, love, affection' (the transition from an adjective to a noun, from a personality attribute to an idea expressing a value is significant) and orange-red signified 'eccentric, active, offensive, aggressive, autonomous, competitive' – hence 'desire, domination, sexuality' (*ibid.*: 232). During the 1940s and 1950s similar experiments were conducted in many American laboratories, among others by Rohrschach, the inventor of the famous Rohrschach inkblot test. A 1972 overview (Pickford, 1972) cites a 1949 study by Warner, which established that men like cool colours and women warmer colours (which corresponds to Goethe's observations) and that neurotics prefer green to yellow (*ibid.*: 234), and a 1953 study by Stapleton in which yellow was associated with 'joy, love, and sexuality', and blue with 'control and mother-centered emotions and attitudes', while red was either positively associated with 'love and the need to be loved', or negatively with 'aggression' – other colours are also part of the study, which strongly stresses the universality of these associations (*ibid.*: 239).

Many contemporary colour advisers continue to work in Goethe's spirit. Colour consultant Lacy (1996) says that red 'activates people to violence within', 'excites our basic tendencies' and 'stimulates action before thought'. 'Theatres, fast food restaurants, bars and casinos are decorated in red', she says, 'so that we may lose track of time when surrounded with this colour' (*ibid.*: 17–18), while 'orange is used by fast food restaurants as they know it creates a friendly atmosphere in which children are welcome. As the colour has a lot of vitality in it customers do not stay long, so it induces a quick turnover' (*ibid.*: 19).

A company called Colour Affects writes in its website:

> As colour has a powerful effect on how we feel, and influences our behaviour, clearly two important applications of colour psychology on interior design are schools and hospitals. Both can be very stressful environments but much can be done with colour to alleviate, for example, worry and fear, and also to enhance concentration, happiness and relaxation. The Colour Affects System for interiors takes account of the relevant psychological modes to create harmonious interiors that support these different needs.

Psychological research on colour has, in fact, changed little in the past 100 years. The same ideas are recycled over and over, yet continue to fascinate the public. An article from *The Independent*, published in February 2009 announces:

> Scientists who monitored the performance of more than 600 people as they underwent a battery of psychological tests found that red stimulated a person's attentiveness, whereas blue fertilized the imagination and inspired a more risk-taking attitude. The researchers found that the study's subjects were unaware of the effect that colour had on their thinking, and suggest that the findings could be used for anything from designing the interior decoration of a school or university to the marketing of products and services.

The central idea continues to be that colour is affective, a direct unmediated feeling, and that colour can have involuntary effects, and it continues to play a key role in Western colour discourse, also in design textbooks, which continue to draw on the work of Bauhaus teachers of the 1920s and 1930s such as Kandinsky and Itten, whose work was strongly influenced by Goethe's legacy. Hornung (2005: 129), for instance, like Goethe, distinguishes 'symbolic colour associations' from 'colour experiences':

> The attachment of the colour blue to the abstraction 'loyalty' is nebulous [and] requires an audience of shared cultural experience . . . If we substitute the word *experience* for meaning, we may get close to the way in which colour can lend significance to form. Colour, when it arouses feeling, tends to do so not as a symbol, but as an analogue. People everywhere seem to equate blue, green and violet with coolness, and red, orange and yellow with warmth . . . This association probably has roots in our longstanding physical relationship to ice, shadows, and deep water (coolness) and to fire, sun and desert (warmth) . . . colour meaning seems to spring from a psychological reaction to physical experience.

Feisner (2006: 120) similarly opens her chapter on colour symbolism by saying 'our emotions influence our perception of colour' and lists meanings such as 'cheerfulness', 'happiness', 'sun', and 'vitality' for yellow, and 'coolness', 'truth' and 'tranquillity' for blue, though she mixes them with more symbolic meanings. Such psychological reactions are, in our society, legitimate emotive reactions to art, and legitimate reasons for choosing colours (where we have a choice). They are sanctioned by the authoritative, expert discourses of psychologists, colour consultants and so on. But they do not apply to the uniforms we might have to wear, or to the colours of traffic lights, or the colour codes of city transport networks. They are not an automatic reaction. We react emotively in contexts where we are licensed, even expected, to do so, and rationally in other contexts.

To sum up, there have been three overlapping trends in the history of European colour meaning. In the Middle Ages, colour played a key role in identifying people, whether biblical figures, saints, monks, knights or outcasts, and in signifying theological and chivalrous ideas and ideals such as 'humility' and 'penitence' or 'loyalty' and 'courtesy'. From the Renaissance onwards, the semiotic landscape became monochrome, and new scientific and naturalistic colour discourses and practices no longer occupied themselves with the question of colour meaning. In the Romantic era, finally, the work of Goethe linked colour to affect, to subjective, individual emotions and personality traits, and to direct, unmediated effects on behaviour. Goethe's ideas were first picked up by painters, and then by psychologists who, in turn, influenced key twentieth-century artists and designers and, later, the field of marketing, with its interest in appealing to the emotions and 'drives' of consumers.

All three trends have remained available as semiotic resources, and in Chapter 7 I will try to show how, today, they mix and reconfigure in new ways to allow colour to express new identities and to inform new, multimodal ways of writing. But before doing so, I will need to explore two further aspects of the way the language of colour has developed: the objective colour systems that scientists and artists developed after Newton, and the language we use to talk about colour. Both are needed to understand how colour operates in today's global culture.

Exercises

1   Which of the three types of meaning discussed in this chapter play a role in the following excerpt from a book on colour for (aspiring) painters by Simon Jennings (2008) and how does Jennings relate them to each other?

> Blue is overwhelmingly present in our lives for it is the colour of the sky, providing an ever-changing backdrop that is echoed and reflected in the sea, rivers, and lakes. From space our planet looks blue. Described by Kandinsky as the 'typical heavenly colour' blue carries a sense of the spiritual. It suggests calmness and serenity in its lighter tones and mystery as it approaches black. In some situations it may convey sadness and melancholy, hence to have 'the blues'. Used in midbright clarity it is an ethereal, expansive colour, while richer blues have velvety depths that evoke opulence and mystique.
>
> . . .
>
> Red is the most dynamic and vibrant colour in the artist's palette. In its purest, saturated form it is the hottest of warm colours. Red is a colour with countless symbolic and contradictory associations in different cultures. It can signify danger, or life; good luck, as well as evil. In India red is the sacred colour of Lakshmi, the goddess of wealth and beauty, and in China a ruby represents longevity. The red planet Mars is named after the Roman god of war. Early physicians wore red robes to signify their healing professions, and doors were painted with a red cross to signify the presence of the bubonic plague.

2   Take colour photos of three objects in which the same colour plays different roles. Ask ten people what the colour of the objects communicates (they could all belong to the same

group, say students or old age pensioners, or to two different groups, e.g. men and women, but they should not be professionally engaged with colour). Relate their answers to the three types of meaning discussed in this chapter, and try to explain why they answer in the way that they do.

3   Choose a colour to symbolize the idea of 'security' and think up different kinds of reasons for your choice. Which kinds of reason do you find most convincing and why?

3 Colour Systems

3.1 Paint as medium and mode

The idea that all colours can be mixed from a small number of primary colours is no longer in question. Without this insight we would have no colour printing, no colour photography, no colour on our computer monitors. But in the past mixing has often been seen as a dubious practice, a kind of contamination, affecting the 'purity' of colour: 'Mixing produces conflict, conflict produces change, and putrefaction is a kind of change', said Plutarch, in the first century AD (quoted in Gage, 1993: 30), and painters of his time praised unmixed colour as 'pure' and 'undefiled' (*ibid.*). What mixing they did was restricted to lightening or darkening, and if colours were mixed at all, the result was considered inferior to unmixed colour. In the words of Alexander of Aphrodisias, a writer from the third century AD (*ibid.*: 31):

> Natural green (*prasinon*) and violet are *chrysocolla* and *ostrum*, the one made from blood and the other sea-purple [a kind of shellfish]. But the artificial colours cannot match them. Green is indeed made from blue (*kuanon*) and tallow (*ochron*) and violet from blue and red, . . . but these artificial colours are far inferior to the natural.

Medieval painters also avoided mixing, especially when paints were made from rare materials or difficult to obtain. I already discussed some examples – purple, made from large quantities of crushed shellfish; red, made from Indian lac and kermes insects; ultramarine, which had to be imported from Afghanistan. Paintings were precious objects, not because they were made by famous artists, but because they used precious materials. Even today, the names of pigments might still refer to their place of origin or manufacturing process, although the paints are no longer imported from India or Afghanistan or made from insects or shellfish, and although the references will be lost to most people.

Around 1600, new types of paint were developed in which each particle of pigment was coated in a film of oil which insulated it against chemical reactions with other pigments that were also present in the medium in which they were suspended. This allowed different coloured particles to keep their own colour in a mixture and made mixing much easier and much more effective. Leonardo da Vinci, like other painters of his time, no longer used unmodulated paint. He reduced his palette to a limited set of primary colours (red, blue, yellow and green, plus white and black) and mixed them to achieve a naturalistic rendering of the play of light and shade and the subtle reflections of colours in shadows. As a result the status of paints as materials went down. Paints were no longer precious. 'Beauty does not mean ultramarine at sixty scudi the ounce', said Paolo Pino, a sixteenth-century Venetian painter (quoted in Gage, 1993: 131). And the purity of unmodulated colour was no longer appreciated. As Ludovico Dolce, another sixteenth-century Venetian said, 'Some painters don't know how to imitate the different nuances of cloth, but put the colours in fully saturated as they stand, so that in their work there is nothing to praise but the colours' (quoted in Gage, 1993: 137). The palette developed, and painters' assistants would systematically set out the colours needed for the highlights and shadows of each primary colour. The modern idea that there is a limited set of primary colours from which all other colours can be mixed was first worked out *in practice* by these artists (some, like Leonardo, also wrote about it), and only later taken up by theorists, who would transform artistic practice into a new theory about the nature of colour – a theory which, in due course, would drive new inventions such as colour printing and colour photography.

The change I have described here exemplifies the difference between what Kress and I, in earlier work (2001), called 'modes' and 'media'. A semiotic *medium* is a type of material substance (e.g. paint or wood) or a type of physical action (e.g. vocalization) that has come into use for purposes of cultural expression and social communication, but in such a way that the materiality of the medium continues to play an important role in communicating meaning, either on the basis of 'provenance' (as in the case of ultramarine) or on the basis of its physical qualities (the lustre of a particular silver paint; the transparency of a particular watercolour; the velvety darkness of a particular black; etc.). To work with a medium, or to understand what colour, used as a medium, conveys, means being responsive to the unique qualities and unique cultural histories of each pigment, each particular colour. As a medium, colour is therefore a more or less unordered collection of material substances, paints, dyes, inks and so on, each with their unique histories and qualities, a 'language', you could say, which only has a vocabulary, and no grammar.

In a semiotic *mode*, on the other hand, meaning is made on the basis of the informal or formal rules of abstract 'systems' or 'grammars'. These rules allow a limited number of elements to create a large number of meanings, in the same way that the system of musical harmony allows an infinite number of musical works to be generated from just 12 tones, or the system of language a very large number of words from just 40 to 70 speech sounds. Once such rules have developed, the mode is no longer associated with one particular materiality, and the words or melodies it generates can be realized in different media, different material forms – a sentence can be materialized as speech or writing, for instance, and a melody can be played by a range of different instruments. It is so also with colour. Once it is conceived of as a system in which a limited number of primary colours are combined into myriad different possible colours by means of a limited set of rules, it is no longer tied to a particular medium. The rules can apply to any medium, to paint or dye as much as to the electronic activation of phosphor dots on television and computer screens (although the primary colours of projected light are not quite the same as those of material media such as paint, dye and ink, as will be explained below). The drawback is that colour, once understood as a mode, might no longer be appreciated for the meanings its materiality can convey, and that, as we will see, is indeed what happened. Yet today, when colour, as seen on computer screens, has lost so much of its materiality and tactility, there is a new hankering for materiality and for the nuances and resonances it can convey.

3.2 The development of modern colour theory

The idea of *primary colours* runs like a thread through the history of colour theory and practice. Strictly speaking, primary colours are colours that cannot be obtained by mixing – red, blue and yellow. More broadly, they are colours that are regarded as fundamental and irreducible in the context of some theory of colour and some way of classifying colours. In early Greek philosophy, many writers posited four primary colours, and related them to the four elements. Even Leonardo still related red to fire, blue to air, green to water and yellow to earth. In the Middle Ages, black, white and red were primary in the sense that they were considered more important than other colours as symbolic colours, and hence more widely discussed and more strictly regulated. In heraldry, too, hierarchies of colour were much debated. Bartolo of Sassoferrato, a fifteenth-century author, saw gold as the noblest colour, because it is the colour of light; red as the next noblest, because it is the colour of the next noblest element, fire; blue as the next noblest because it is the colour of air; white as next noblest, because it is light; and black as least noble, because it is opposed to white.

The modern theory of primary colours was triggered by the new appreciation of colour mixing. Leonardo's primary colours were red, yellow, green and blue (he saw black and white as colours too) and they could be mixed to generate secondary colours as follows:

Red + Yellow = Orange
Yellow + Green = Yellow-Green
Green + Blue = Blue-Green
Blue + Red = Purple

The modern *subtractive* system of colour mixing (see Figure 3.1), that is, the system for mixing coloured substances such as paints and dyes (as opposed to mixing coloured light beams) stems directly from this. The typical modern version has three primary colours, red, yellow and blue, which can be mixed to generate three *secondary colours* as follows:

Red + Blue = Purple
Red + Yellow = Orange
Blue + Yellow = Green

Tertiary colours are then mixtures of a primary and a secondary colour – yellow-orange, orange-red, and so on. When all three primaries are mixed together, the result is a muddy black.

In Figure 3.2 each secondary colour is adjacent to the colours from which it is mixed and opposite its *complementary colour*. Complementary colours are the colours which include the other primary or primaries, e.g. the complementary colour of the primary colour red is green, the mixture of the other two primaries (yellow and blue), and the complementary colour of purple, which mixes the primaries blue and red, is yellow, the one primary it does not contain in itself. Complementary colours also appear in afterimages. When staring intently at a colour, say green, and then closing your eyes, an 'afterimage' of the complementary colour red will be 'seen' (see Figure 3.3).

The theory achieved more or less its current form in the writings of the English painter Moses Harris (1731–85), who added two further aspects of colour, *value* (which he called 'intensity') and *saturation*. As a result of Newton's discovery of the prismatic colours, black and white had begun to be regarded, not as colours, but as modifications of colour, as different degrees of the lightness or darkness of any given colour, hence as a separate dimension, the dimension *value* (or, as it is sometimes also called, 'brightness'). Figure 3.4 shows nine values of 12 primary, secondary and tertiary colours, with the 'pure' colours connected into a circle.

The second aspect he added was *saturation*, the degree of purity of a colour. Different degrees of saturation are best imagined as different degrees to which grey (or a complementary) is mixed in with the colour, keeping it equally light or dark, but gradually more muted, until it becomes what is sometimes called a 'chromatic grey', a grey in which a tinge of colour can only just be detected, and finally an 'achromatic grey', a colourless grey. Different levels of saturation can be seen in Figure 3.5.

Harris worked with 18 hues, 20 levels of value and 20 levels of saturation, generating 660 different colours (although he used only 33 colour names), and he was also the first to display these colours on a 'colour wheel', though his was considerably more complex than the colour wheel shown in Figure 3.2.

Philip Runge, a German painter (1777–1810), was the first to display a colour system in three dimensions – as a sphere in which the hues are displayed along the equator, and the values along the vertical axis, so that the north pole is white, and the south pole black, with the different values of each hue running from north to south, from light to dark. The centre of the sphere is grey, so that the line that runs from each pure hue to the centre moves towards increasingly muted colours, ending up in a grey from which all colour is drained. Again, the colours are so arranged on the sphere's equator that each colour is opposite its complementary. For Runge, this system did not merely classify and order the world of colour, it also expressed a divine order. Harking back to medieval symbolism, he saw his primary colours as the colours of the Trinity (blue for the Father, red for the Son, and yellow for the Holy Spirit), and he saw black as the colour of darkness and evil, and white as the colour of light and goodness (Fischer, 1996).

Albert Munsell (1858–1918), an American painter and colour theorist, refined this into a colour system that is still in use today, using the same three-dimensional architecture, but discerning five primary hues ('principal colours'), Yellow, Red, Green, Blue and Purple, with the following complementaries (see Figure 3.6).

Yellow – Blue-Purple
Red – Blue-Green
Green – Red-Purple
Blue – Orange
Purple – Yellow-Green

Munsell then added a numerical system. On a scale of ten steps from light to dark, the pure colours, on the surface of the equator, were 5 plus a letter indicating the colour (e.g. pure yellow was 5Y) and intermediate colours were given intermediate numbers, so that a colour halfway between red and orange would be 10R (see Figure 3.7). Value was expressed by an additional number, on a scale of 10, so that 5R9 would be a very pale pink. Saturation was expressed by yet another number, on a scale measured in equal steps from neutral grey to the greatest saturation each hue could have at a particular value, e.g. 5R5/14 is a middle value pure red. Munsell's *Colour Atlas*, originally published in 1915, and republished as *The Munsell Book of Colour* in 1929, was adopted by the American Standards Association and is still widely used for specifying colour, for instance in dye and paint manufacturing, interior design, the production of cosmetics, and computer software.

This did not end the debate about primaries and mixing. The chemist Wilhelm Ostwald (1853–1932), for instance, reintroduced green as a primary, arguing for psychological primaries, colours *perceived* as irreducible, rather than basing himself on 'mixability'. He rejected the spectrum as a source because it has no black and cannot generate duller colours such as brown and olive green, which nevertheless figure importantly in the human environment. And he also considered black a colour, because, he said, we can measure its sensation (see Scott-Taylor, 1935). As Arnheim has said (1974: 340):

The question of which colours can produce all others by mixture is not the same as the question of which colours are perceived as simple and irreducible, and much of the differences between the various systems relate to these different questions and the different purposes behind them.

Modern painters often devise their own 'primaries', their unique palette, rather than the well-ordered palettes which the Renaissance painters had introduced. Van Gogh's self-portrait of 1888 shows him with a palette containing mostly orange, red, blue and green, still close to the traditional primaries. Matisse's palette of 1937, as described by Gage (1993: 188),

> shows a setting of 17 colours, running in what seems like an arbitrary sequence from peach-black at the thumbhole to madderlake, with several cadmium yellows and reds, cadmium purple and lemon-yellow, yellow and brown ochres, two cobalt-violets, dark ultramarine, viridian and two mixed greens. In the centre are placed large mounds of white.

Clearly Matisse no longer followed the traditional system and let himself be guided by the material qualities of colour – he was interested in colour as 'retinal sensation' and in the 'tactile vitality' of colour (Matisse, 1973: 58).

As mentioned, modern colour theory derived from the practices of painters, but colour printing and colour photography would turn out to need quite different primaries. Jacques Christophe LeBlon (1667–1742), the inventor of colour printing, initially thought red, yellow and blue would be able to generate all other colours, but soon found that this idea did not quite work in practice and that less pure colours mixed better – his yellow, for instance, was in fact a 'vegetable brown pink' (Gage, 1993: 16). In contemporary CMYK printing, the 'primaries' are Cyan, Magenta and Yellow (the 'K' in CMYK stands for 'key', black), producing secondary colours as follows:

Yellow + Cyan = Green
Cyan + Magenta = Purple
Magenta + Yellow = Orange

This generates the following tertiary colours – paradoxically red and blue become tertiary colours here!

Yellow + Green = Yellow-Green
Green + Cyan = Green-Blue-Green
Cyan + Violet = Blue
Violet + Magenta = Red-Violet-Red
Magenta + Orange = Red
Orange + Yellow = Yellow-Orange

Three-colour prints are made with three different plates, containing the yellow, magenta and cyan images in patterns of tiny dots, as shown in Figure 3.8. The dots of a three-colour print can be seen in enlargement, but at normal size the eye cannot separate them and they appear to fuse together in single mixed colours – they 'mix optically'. Printers rely on the so-called PMS system (Pantone Matching System) which has nine colours plus black and transparent white, together with recipes that stipulate, for instance, for a particular pink: 1½ parts Pantone Rhod Red, ½ part Pantone Warm Red, and 14 parts Pantone Transparent Red, allowing printers to mix inks to produce the exact required colour.

In the case of projected images, the principle is quite different, because they use additive, rather than subtractive mixing (see Figure 3.1). Blue, green and red light, mixed in equal proportions, produces white light. Blue, green and red are therefore the *additive primaries*. Modern data projectors, for instance, produce three beams of light, a red, a green and a blue one, and all other colours can be mixed from these three. The nineteenth-century physicist Hermann von Helmholtz (1821–94) first described the difference between subtractive and additive colour mixing, demonstrating that projected colours are more intense and possess greater saturation than reflected colours, because they are mixed additively, with each additional colour adding light and bringing the whole a step closer to white, while, in subtractive mixing, each additional colour takes light away, and brings the whole a step closer to black. Maxwell (1831–79) demonstrated that secondary colours can be mixed additively from red, green and blue to obtain cyan, magenta and yellow as follows:

Red + Blue = Magenta
Red + Green = Yellow
Green + Blue = Cyan

These discoveries were fundamental for the development of colour photography. To understand how colour film works it is necessary to understand the effect of filters. Filters of a certain colour filter out their complementaries. Thus a cyan filter lets green and blue pass, but filters out red (lips will become very dark, as in early black and white movies, which were not sensitive to red); a yellow filter lets red and green pass, but filters out blue, so that, for instance, skies will become very dark; and a magenta filter lets red and blue pass, but filters out green so green objects become very dark. Photographic film consists of three layers, with filters in between. The first layer is sensitive only to blue light, so registers all the blue parts of the subject. Then a yellow filter screens out the blue, so that only red and green can pass to the second layer, which is sensitive to blue and green light, but registers only the green parts of the subject, because blue light has already been filtered out. Then a red filter screens out blue and green, and lets only red pass to the final layer. Each layer contains the complementary pigments. Red becomes cyan, green magenta and blue yellow. This is because photographic emulsion registers a negative image in which light becomes dark and dark light. When this negative is re-photographed, a negative of the negative – in other words a positive – results.

On computer and television screens red, blue and green phosphor dots are activated by electronic signals and then 'optically mixed', resulting in the illusion of a full colour image, much as in colour printing.

3.3 The materiality of colour

As we have seen, modern colour theory conceives of colour as a 'mode', an abstract, generative system of hues, modified by value and saturation. This pushes the material qualities of specific colour substances into the background, even though in earlier times they had often been considered more important than hue. Yet they have never gone away. They continued to be noticed and appreciated, even while they were marginalized. And in recent times they have begun to be re-valued. Almost 100 years ago, the Russian art critic Tarabukin argued that 'material colours themselves have an autonomous aesthetic value which is not exhausted by hue' and compared them to the timbre of musical instruments, which stems directly from the materials they are made of. Modern artists, said Tarabukin, draw attention to the materiality of their materials 'which are no longer the inferior element they were for the masters of the past' (quoted in Gage, 1993: 225). More recently the Italian designer and architect Alessandro Mendini also stressed the materiality of colour (quoted in Koolhaas *et al.*, 2001: 238):

> Colour can become material, very often superficial at first sight. But other colours can be massive, heavy: a block of basalt is black, entirely. Therefore, as I work increasingly as an architect, I try to be careful about the relation between colour and material: in the transparency of glass, for instance, in its translucency, its being matt or lustrous or wrinkled, its systems of veining.

Some of these qualities are discussed below.

Luminosity and luminescence

The luminosity of a colour lies in its ability to glow from within. Lighter and more strongly saturated colours are more luminous, but the impression of luminosity also depends on the surrounding colours. Painters enhance it by surrounding intense, light colours with less intense, darker colours, perhaps in complementary hues, for instance the orange light of the sun reflected in water, surrounded by dark blue water, as in Monet's *Le Soleil dans le Brouillard* (1904).

Luminosity, or 'brilliance', as it is also referred to, has often been valued highly, as in Pliny's praise of purple (quoted in Gage, 1993: 25):

> that precious colour which gleams with the hue of a dark rose . . . This is the purple for which the Roman fasces and axes clear a way. It is the badge of noble youth; it distinguishes the senator from the knight; it is called in to appease the Gods. It brightens every garment and shares with God the glory of the triumph.

Love of brilliance also characterized medieval attitudes to colour. In the Middle Ages, the colour of Christ's robe was chosen, not on the basis of hue, but of luminosity. It did not matter whether that robe was red, gold or white, so long as it was luminous. No doubt, luminosity is a key aspect of ceremonial splendour in many cultures, as was already noted by Marco Polo, who described the palace of the Gran Kaan as follows (quoted in Eco, 2002: 108):

> The roof is varnished in vermillion, green, blue, yellow and all the other colours; and so well and cunningly is this done, that it glitters like crystal, and can be seen shining from a great way all around.

Luminescent colour glows or radiates either because it is lit from behind, as in the case of painted glass, or coloured neon light, or because it is itself a source of light, as in gasflames or the glow of radiators.

Lustre and iridescence

The lustre ('sheen', 'gloss') of a colour results not from the transmission or emission of coloured light, but from the reflectiveness of coloured surfaces. Painters suggest reflective surfaces by using highlights and shading them in the colours of the surrounding objects whose colours the surfaces reflect. But using colour to suggest lustre is not the same as actually using lustrous colours. Like luminosity, lustre has long been a key aspect of the most highly prized colours, such as gold and purple. In the empress Theodora's robe at Ravenna (*c*.540) 'it was probably the shine, not the hue, which proclaimed its true Imperial Purple' (Gage, 1993: 55).

Iridescence creates a 'shimmer'. It results from movement, making objects seem to glitter as their movement, or the viewer's movement, changes the angle of vision. It was – and perhaps still is – particularly important in mosaics, where, for instance, the little cubes of the haloes of Saints would be angled for extra shininess and where 'a chequerboard type of shading gave an optical shimmer to soft or lustrous subjects' (Gage, 1993: 50). After all, 'the hall of God' needed to 'shine with its mosaics' to make 'the precious light of faith gleam even more brightly' (*ibid.*: 46). In Byzantine churches, the movement of the spectator helped create sparkle and shimmer. Even in the fifteenth century, sparkle and gloss were still important, and paintings might be ornamented with real jewels and gold to achieve it (*ibid.*: 199). Architect Mendini connects iridescence to modern 'electronic colour' (quoted in Koolhaas *et al.*, 2001: 241):

> When I was thinking about the Groninger Museum, a vision that I have is that of making a flower, or similarly, a fish or insect or bird. . . . Tropical fish . . . may have an iridescent colour, as well as a reflecting and fluorescent colour . . . so that when the fish is deep down, you can only see parts of it but not the whole. As far as Groningen is concerned, . . . for this building too, the flower concept played a part.

Transparency and translucency

A colour is transparent when light passes through it so that things in the background can be seen behind things in the foreground, as in the case of watercolour or coloured wood stain. This melts the colour with the materiality of its carrier, lying over it like a transparent film, which can make the colour less substantial, more ethereal.

Translucent objects partially block the light that passes through them, making background objects soft and vague, as if seen through a veil or gauze. Leonardo da Vinci, discovered that distant objects become lighter and more similar in hue and value, and therefore softened the contours and the colours of his backgrounds.

Temperature

The idea that colours on the red end of the spectrum are 'warmer' than colours at the blue end of the spectrum, is now commonplace. Colour 'temperature' is also used to create an illusion of distance, with distant, 'receding' objects gradually getting bluer, and close, 'advancing' objects redder. Albers (1975[1963]) pointed out that reading the warmth of a colour depends on its environment – there is an 'influenced' and an 'influencing' colour. For Arnheim (1974: 328–9) temperature was not just a matter of hue, but also influenced by value and saturation. It is difficult to call isolated pure colours 'warm' or 'cold', he said. The effect is reached by 'deviation' – a bluish red is colder than a reddish blue:

> Perhaps it is not so much the dominant hue, but its 'afflictions' that produce the expressive quality. Perhaps the basic hues are fairly neutral key values distinguished by

their being unique and mutually exclusive, rather than by their specific expression, and it is only when a colour produces a dynamic tension effect by leaning towards another colour that it reveals its expressive characteristics.

Texture

The term texture is used to cover a range of colour qualities such as transparency and lustre, but also actual textural qualities that influence colour, such as roughness and smoothness. Rougher textures make colours seem darker and warmer, while 'smooth, shiny surfaces are usually rendered in a cool temperature' (Feisner, 2006: 89). Impressionist painters were newly interested in the materiality of paint, using rough canvas and stiff paints to create visible brush strokes, and ever since then, texture, the materiality of the materials used by artists, has continued to play a role in art.

Although textbooks for artists and designers usually mention at least some of these aspects of colour, colour theory has marginalized them and they are not represented on key visual representations of the system of colour, such as colour wheels and colour spheres. This focus on constructing semiotic resources as 'modes', and on abstracting away from materiality and its expressive potential, is not restricted to the field of colour. It has been a tendency of thought in other areas as well. Linguists have favoured grammars that abstract away from the materiality of speech, handwriting and typography. Musicological theory has focused on harmony, abstracting away from the timbres of specific voices and musical instruments. It will be one of the aims of this book to reintegrate these material aspects of colour into colour theory and to show how they contribute to contemporary cultural expression and social communication.

3.4 Colour harmony

So far we have looked at the qualities of individual colours, and the way they are mixed. But colours usually come in combinations in which they interact and affect each other. As Ruskin said (quoted in Arnheim, 1974: 354):

> Every hue is altered by every touch that you add in other places; so that what was warm a minute ago, becomes cold when you have put a hotter colour in another place, and what was in harmony when you left it, becomes discordant as you set other colours beside it.

Colour interaction began to be systematically explored by Renaissance artists who sought to improve their ability to produce the illusion of three-dimensional space in two-dimensional works. Leonardo discovered that complementary colours influence each other: ' Colours will appear what they are not, according to the ground which surrounds them' (quoted in Feisner, 20067: 13). And he realized that the modelling and shading of objects was not just a matter of grading the value of the same colour, but also of blending different colours. The modelling and shading techniques pioneered in this period continue to be used today. Highlights (see Figure 3.9) will be tinted, not with a lighter version of the same colour, but with a very light version of the nearest primary, e.g. the highlight of a red object will be a very pale blue. Reflected shadows will contain the colour of the object itself as well as that of the neighbouring surfaces. If, for instance, an object is orange, and placed on a green surface, the 'light area' will be a lighter value of orange, the 'form shading' a darker value of orange, while the 'form shadow' will be darker still, and less saturated, with some green mixed in. The 'reflected shadow' will add further, and less saturated green, while the 'cast shadow' will be a dull green with orange in it, getting weaker towards the edges (see Feisner, 2006: 41). To this the effect of illumination should be added. Artificial light is warmer than daylight, and the colour of daylight varies with the time of the day and the weather.

Colour can also help create an illusion of depth. Foreground colours will be warmer and more saturated, background colours colder, less saturated and more homogeneous in hue and value. And then there is the use of colour to create textural effects – the use of highlights and transparency in painting water, or the use of hue, saturation and colour contrast to render the reflectivity of metal surfaces. All these aspects of colour interaction have a single aim – increasing the illusion of three-dimensionality and texturality in two-dimensional, flat images.

Some of these discoveries would, much later, be theorized in the work of Michel Chevreul (1786–1889), a French tapestry manufacturer who found that his colours often did not work, not because of the dyes he used, but because of the influence of other, adjacent colours. He concluded that 'two adjacent colours, when seen by the eye, will appear as dissimilar as possible' (quoted in Fischer, 1996: 73), the so-called 'law of simultaneous contrast' which Leonardo had already observed and which Goethe had also drawn attention to – looking at the same red, first on a yellow background, then on a violet background, you will see two different reds. The first will be darkened, the second will look orange. In other words, opposing, complementary colours intensify each other, and non-complementary colours 'contaminate' each other (e.g. a yellow next to a green will acquire a tinge of violet). This discovery, too, was put in the service of pictorial representation, as it inspired painters to suggest forms by resonance and contrast of colour, rather than through line drawing. I will discuss this further in Chapter 6.

The colour interactions explored by these painters were still in the service of representation, even though the Impressionists' idea of 'recording sensations', of painting things as we subjectively see them, differed from the naturalism of the Renaissance which sought to paint things as we objectively are. But in abstract art, and in modern colour theory, the emphasis lies, not on using colour interaction for purposes of representation, but on more formal and aesthetic ideas about what colours go together and why – on abstract theories of 'colour harmony'. Most were based on the colour wheel, and therefore only on hue, and especially on complementariness. As Goethe had already observed, complementary colours harmonize well. Blue goes well with orange, red with green, yellow with purple (see Figure 3.2), and so on. Variations include the 'Double Complementary Colour Scheme' which has two sets of complementary hues, e.g. blue and orange as well as green and red, and the 'Split Complementary Scheme' which combines any hue with two hues on each side of its complementary, for instance red with yellow-green and blue-green. Then there is the 'Harmony of Adjacents' – three or more hues that are located next to each other on a colour wheel, for instance yellow-orange, orange and red, and the 'Triad Colour Scheme' of three colours that are equidistant from each other on the wheel, e.g. yellow, orange and red, or yellow, red and blue (this will always lead to a bias for either 'warm', or 'cool' colours).

Wilhelm Ostwald was the first to suggest that colour harmony might also be based on value or saturation, for instance in 'monochromatic harmonies', harmonies of different values of the same colour (Scott-Taylor, 1935). He favoured colour schemes of four different values of two complementary colours (e.g. green and red) and equidistant triads (which are always also complementary). His ideas influenced Johannes Itten (1970: 19) who added the concept of 'modulation': 'One principal hue and many variant tints and shades'. Modulation, according to Itten, involves three dimensions – temperature (cool/warm), value (light/dark), and saturation (dull/intense). More generally, he argued that any contrast could become a principle for generating colour schemes: 'Two or more colours in order to harmonize must be equal with regard to essential elements' (quoted in Arnheim, 1974: 347). Munsell (1969) also based his view of colour harmony on the principle of common elements. He saw the centre of his colour sphere (see Figure 3.6) as the balancing point for all colours, so that any straight line through that centre would automatically connect harmonizing colours.

More recent theorists pointed out that in music harmony implies dissonance. Much of the interest and 'drama' of European music comes from the to and fro between dissonance and consonance. Might not colour harmony be based on a similar principle, for instance by puncturing a set of harmonizing colours with a single anomalous colour that stands out as different and dissonant and adds spice to the whole? To Arnheim (1974: 348), colour harmony based on the principle of similarity and concordance is

> the most primitive kind of harmony, suitable at best for the colour schemes of nurseries and baby clothing . . . A colour composition based on nothing but such a common denominator could describe only a world of absolute peace, devoid of action, static in mood. It would represent a state of deadly serenity in which, to borrow the physicist's language, entropy approaches an absolute minimum.

Clash and discord, disturbing the balance, is not a bad thing, Arnheim said (*ibid.*: 355), so long as it fits the overall structure of the work.

The influential colour theorist Albers also criticized the traditional approach to colour harmony (Albers, 1975[1963]: 42):

> We may forget for a while those rules of thumb of complementaries, whether complete or 'split', and of triads and tetrads as well. They are worn out . . . No mechanical colour system is flexible enough to precalculate the manifold changing factors, as named before, in a single recipe. Good painting, good colouring is comparable to good cooking. Even a good cooking recipe demands tasting and repeated tasting while it is being followed. And the best tasting still depends on a cook with taste. By giving up preference for harmony, we accept dissonance to be as desirable as consonance.

And yet this approach is still widely taught. Feisner (2006: 66), for instance, recommends 'rhythmically distributing' different colours in order to create 'coherence' and 'unity', with equal 'balance' between sunlight and shadow, or, in a more abstract context, light and dark, warm and cold, and so on. The ultimate aim is 'creating order', being 'pleasing', not 'disturbing' (*ibid.*: 44–5):

> A composition of few hues is generally more pleasing than one of many. A composition of few hues that are executed in many values tends to be even more pleasing.

Only when 'emphasis' is needed, 'the creation of areas of importance for the viewer to focus upon' (*ibid.*: 72), can the harmony be disturbed to some degree. Here, Feisner recommends that dominant (highly saturated) hues should be used, and they should contrast with less dominant (less saturated) hues in their immediate environment. Other textbooks are more open-minded and allow students to explore both harmony and dissonance. Hornung (2005: 97ff.) recommends exercises to explore the following principles for creating colour schemes: 'colours with a lot in common', 'any two colours', 'two disparate colours (together with a set of colours that "bridge" them)', and 'colour anomaly (introducing a colour that runs counter to the consistency of the whole'). He also recommends creating a colour scheme by inventorizing the colours of some object, whether natural (e.g. autumn leaves) or human-made (e.g. a Byzantine mosaic).

To sum up, modern colour theory sees colour as combining three dimensions, hue, value and saturation. Yet its main focus is on hue, on classifying and hierarchizing colours into 'pure' and mixed colours, and on devising systems of colour harmony on this basis. In the process, material aspects of colour such as luminosity and lustre were marginalized – a marginalization which, arguably, has continued in twentieth-century technology, with its dematerialization of colour on the screens of computer monitors and mobile phones. Despite this, twentieth-century artists, postmodern philosophers and cultural theorists have re-ignited interest in the materiality of colour.

In all this, however, there has been a complete disjuncture, a complete lack of integration, between modern colour theory, the currently dominant theory of colour form, and colour psychology, the currently dominant theory of colour meaning. The terminology of the colour theory discussed in this chapter is entirely formal and aesthetic, and classifies colour and aspects of colour without any regard for what colour communicates and how. To a semiotician this is untenable. A theory of colour must be able to connect form and meaning, must be able to account for the way colour resources and their uses are socially structured to enable the kind of cultural expression and social communication society needs. It is this I will attempt in this book. But before attempting to do so, one further aspect needs to be discussed, the difference between the colour theory developed by artists and scientists and the way we talk about colour in everyday life. It is this I will do in the next chapter.

Exercises

1 What view of colour harmony lies behind this exegesis of El Greco's *The Virgin with Sta. Ines and Sta. Tecla* (1597–99) (Figure 3.10) by Rudolf Arnheim (1974: 367)?

> The self-contained oval shape of the Virgin is subdivided into four main sections, which produce a kind of central symmetry around the Christ child. The two parts of the blue coat oppose each other, and so do those of her red dress. The blue and the red are clearly distinct from each other, but also connected, since the red is somewhat bluish and the blue somewhat reddish. The colour range of the Virgin is kept within the areas of red and blue and therefore requires completion. The missing yellow is supplied by the hair of the child. The child has the role of a keystone, not only because of his central location, but also because he holds the color that is needed to create the triad of primaries.

> The yellow hair of the four child angels at Mary's feet is related by similarity to the yellow coat and hair of the saint at the left, the palm branch, and the lion. The blue of the Virgin's coat is picked up by the blue sleeve. The blue and red of the upper figure add up to a purple, and purple and green approach complementarity. Hence the easy union between the central figure and the woman at the left. Compare this with the clash between the orange coat of the woman at the right and the purple scheme of the Virgin. The red, dominant in both areas, is torn into the conflicting scales of red-blue and red-yellow, and the barrier created by this clash prevents the eye from gliding across the interval between the two figures.

In the original painting there is enough of a golden tinge in the shadows of the yellow coat at the left to prevent a true clash between it and the orange red of the coat at the right. The eye can connect the colours by structural inversion, just as the contact of the two frontal hands, the parallelism of the other two hands, the symmetrical shape of the two-woman group, and the 'peacable kingdom' theme of lion and lamb all strengthen the horizontal tie.

In sum, we find that in the lower half of El Greco's painting, shape and colour combine in representing two united aspects of the religious attitude, inspiration and contemplation, receiving and meditating, dependence upon grace and freedom of will. The overall symmetry of the work makes the contrast of the two-fold human attitude fit into the greater harmony of godhead and man, dominance on high and submission on earth.

2   Find examples of four of the colour schemes mentioned in this chapter and find two applications each of luminosity, lustre and translucency in contemporary fashion or designed objects.

3   Design a colour scheme (at least ten colours) with an element of dissonance and explain what applications it might be used for.

4 Colour Names

4.1 The question of colour names

In the mid-nineteenth century, the English statesman and classical scholar William Gladstone found himself puzzled by the colour words in Homer's epic poems, which were written between 700 and 650 BC. The goddess Hera was described as 'grey-eyed', but the word for 'grey' (*glaucos*) was also used to describe the colour of willows and olives. The sea was sometimes 'yellow-grey', at other times 'wine-red'. The word *leukos* ('white'), described a wide range of things we do not normally call white, for instance water, metallic surfaces and the sun, and the word *chloron* was used for green as well as yellow things, for leaves as well as for honey and sand. From such examples Gladstone concluded that the 'the origin of colour and its impressions were but partially developed among the Greeks of the heroic age' (quoted in Berlin and Kay, 1991: 135). In other words, he thought that the Greeks of this period were colourblind; that they could not differentiate between colours in the way we can today.

Not everyone agreed. Grant Allen, writing in 1879, argued that a limited colour vocabulary, in which the same word can apply to different colours, does not mean that these different colours are not actually perceived (quoted in Berlin and Kay, 1991: 137):

> Mr Gladstone tells us that the Homeric Greeks could not have understood real colours by their apparent colour terms, because the words are used so loosely. Here green means green. There it means fresh or young. So be it. Has Mr Gladstone never heard of red blood, red skies, red brick, or red Indians? Do Englishmen ever talk of green old age or Americans of green corn, which is really pale yellow? . . . Are not colour terms always vague, and are they not vaguer in the language of poetry than anywhere else?

Gladstone had assumed that all things have a single, specific colour. Grass is green. Water is blue. Snow is white. Allen, like painters and poets before him, argued that the colours of grass and water and snow can depend on the time of day, the kind of light that falls on them and the colour of the objects that surround them 'How sharp is the eye which notes the almost imperceptible tinge of greenness in the face of fear, and likens it at once to the full green of grass' (*ibid.*).

Around the same time, Hugo Magnus, a German ophthalmologist, conducted ethnographic research among the Ovahero in South-West Africa, to prove that colour naming and colour perception are two different things, and that 'primitive' people see colour in exactly the same way as 'civilized' people. When it comes to practical matters such as the colours of livestock, Magnus observed, 'primitive' people have no difficulty in naming colours. But when they have no practical reason for naming colours, they do not see a need to express themselves precisely, and may use 'yellow' (i.e. the pale yellow of cattle) for green as well as for blue, or use words which are not colour words at all, e.g. 'lemon' instead of 'yellow' (quoted in Berlin and Kay, 1991: 148):

> Just as we say 'lemon yellow', various tribes in West and South Africa used the same comparison and called yellow *abonua*, i.e. lemon. An expression similar to our 'straw yellow' is found among the natives of Gippsland (Australia) as well. Moreover, the names of various other fruits which are of an intense yellow colouring or which are used in making yellow dye, and the names of yellow animals such as giraffes, butterflies, etc., are all employed for the designation of 'yellow'.

These early writings set the scene for a debate on colour naming that continues today, and is still dominated by the same issues – the difference between colour naming and colour perception which was first studied by Magnus, and the different ways in which colours are classified in different contexts, hinted at by Allen ('Here green means green. There it means fresh or young') and further elaborated by anthropologists, for instance in Conklin's famous study of colour words among the Hanuhóo, a people from the Philippines (Conklin, 1964). As Conklin explains, the Hanuhóo word *latuy* is used for light green and mixtures of green, yellow and brown and the word *rara* covers red and reddish brown. Does this mean that the Hanuhóo cannot see the difference between green, yellow and brown? No, because *latuy* and *rara* are not just colour words. *Latuy* also means 'wet' and 'fresh', and *rara* also means 'dry'. Bamboo, though brown, can be 'green' when it is newly cut, shiny and wet, and 'red' when it is dried out and matured. In other words, the Hanuhóo classify and name colours, not on the basis of colour perception, but on the basis of their interest in plant life, just as the Ovahero colour vocabulary was based on their interest in tending livestock. In classifying and naming colours, people might use the same word for a number of different colours because objects of that colour have some other common characteristic that is more important to them (e.g. 'wetness'), or they might use different colour words (e.g. for distinguishing the many colours of cattle) where other languages only have one. They do so on the basis of what matters to them, on the basis of *interest*, 'that complex condensation of cultural and social histories and awareness of present contingencies' (Kress and Van Leeuwen, 2006: 12). In the case of the Hanuhóo, their interest in plant life structured their colour vocabulary, in the case of the Tzoltzil-speaking Mayan weavers in Mexico studied by MacKeigan and Muth (2006), it was, at least in part, their awareness of ancient Mayan uses of colour coding in measuring space and time in which white stood for 'north', yellow for 'south', red for 'east' and black for 'west'. Contemporary Western culture is no different. We, too, might use a single word for a range of colours. The colour of 'white' wine, for instance, might actually be a golden amber or a pale, almost pinkish white, and the faces of 'white' people can be quite red, or yellow. And we, too, might use a range of colour names where others have only a single word if our many professional specializations or our interest in individual lifestyle choices and unique corporate branding requires it. Arnheim (1974: 345) quotes a chart of colour names which lists eight different names for one and the same colour: orange chrome, golden poppy, spectrum orange, bitter sweet orange, oriental red, Saturn red, cadmium red orange, and red orange.

When describing colours, on the other hand, we focus, not on what we see as the stable, constant colour of things, but on their momentary appearances, on that instability which is perhaps the reason why the colour words and colour classifications of so many languages are not based on hue, but on apparently less fleeting, less ephemeral qualities of people, places and things. Nevertheless, as we will see in the next section, the study of colour names has been profoundly and decisively influenced by a book which largely ignored both nuances of this kind and specific cultural interests, focusing instead on classificatory colour vocabularies: *Basic Colour Terms*, by Berlin and Kay (1991).

4.2 Berlin and Kay

The American linguist Benjamin Whorf, who studied native American languages in the 1930s and 40s, concluded from his studies that their vocabularies and grammars embodied a wholly different way of thinking about the world. In the Hopi language, for instance, there is no noun for 'wave'. Concepts such as 'wave' and 'spray' can only be expressed as verbs, in constructions that would translate as 'it (e.g. a fountain) sprays' or 'it (e.g. a liquid) waves' (Whorf, 1993[1956]: 53). Nor does Hopi have nouns for time concepts such as 'September', 'morning' or 'sunset'. The nearest English rendering of Hopi time expressions would be as adverbs. Hopi would say something like 'He hunts summer-now' *(ibid.*: 143). This, Whorf argued, results in a wholly different way of thinking. The English language objectifies dynamic processes, and for this reason we can think about processes in the same way as we think about objects. We can, for instance, attribute qualities to time. We can think of summer as *being* hot, whereas Hopi would have to think of summer as being *'when we feel* hot', i.e. of heat as a subjective experience, rather than as an objective quality of 'summer'. We can also count time, 'count the days', 'waste five hours', 'use the Summer', and so on, none of which would make sense to the Hopi who can only think of time as 'becoming later and later'. As Whorf explains it (*ibid.*: 151):

> Unvarying repetition is not wasted . . . It is as if the return of the day were felt as the return of the same person, a little older, but with all the impressions of yesterday, not as 'another day', i.e. like an entirely different person.

To Whorf, and others, 'language death', the loss of small languages, is an intellectual loss, a loss of different, sometimes better, ways of thinking about the natural world and the environment we live in. The same applies to the colour vocabularies of other cultures. They offer different ways of thinking about colour, and can challenge the colour theories which, though only a few hundred years old, are now accepted as unassailable scientific truth in the Western world. Whorf's views eventually came to be known as the theory of linguistic relativity, the view that differences between cultures are reflected in, and fed by, differences between their languages. However, the study that started a wave of research into colour naming, Berlin and Kay's *Basic Colour Terms* (1991), first published in 1969, disagreed with the linguistic relativity thesis, and hypothesized a universal colour-naming system. The apparent differences between different cultures, Berlin and Kay argued, is only due to the fact that different cultures are at different stages in a universal pattern of the evolution of colour vocabularies.

According to Berlin and Kay there are 11 basic colour categories – white, black, red, green, yellow, blue, brown, purple, pink, orange and grey. From a study of 98 languages, they drew the following conclusions:

- All languages contain a term for 'black' and a term for 'white'.

- If a language has three colour terms, the third is always red.

- If there are four terms, the fourth is always green or yellow.

LIBRARY, UNIVERSITY OF CHESTER

- If there are five terms, the language will have both green and yellow.

- If there are six terms, the sixth is blue.

- If there are seven terms, the seventh is brown.

- If there are eight terms, there will be a term for either purple, pink, orange or grey.

They saw this as an evolutionary process. In a first stage, there is only black and white. Then red is added – and used also for what we would call yellow, brown, pink and purple. Then yellow or green is added, used also for what we could call blue-green, blue and purple. And so on, until the eighth stage is reached and all 11 basic colours are named.

Like most colour-name researchers, Berlin and Kay used a wide range of anthropological evidence to support their theory. As evidence for the evolutionary first stage, for instance, they quoted the anthropologist Koch who had studied the Jalé in New Guinea, and reported that they had only two colour words, *sing* for 'black' and *hóló* for 'white', plus some terms that were only used in very specific contexts, e.g. *mut* for 'red soil' and *pianó* for a particular plant they used to create a green dye. When Koch used the word *pianó* to refer to the colour of an object other than that plant, the Jalé misunderstood him. When he called the colour of the plant *sing* or *hóló*, depending on the brightness of the green, he *was* understood, so Berlin and Kay reported (1991: 24).

To reach their conclusions, Berlin and Kay not only consulted the anthropological literature, they also interviewed speakers from a wide range of languages who, however, all lived in California. They asked these informants to list the basic colour words in their language and to circle the areas to which those words apply on a colour chart based on the Munsell sphere (see Figure 3.6). They then 'normalized' their data as follows:

- Only simple 'mono-lexemic' words were considered, i.e. terms with suffixes such as '-ish', '-coloured' etc., and compounds such as 'light blue' or 'deep green' were ruled out.

- Only terms that were not restricted to limited domains were included, e.g. 'blonde' would be excluded because it is only used for the colour of hair.

- Only terms which do not also designate objects (terms without 'obvious designation') were included.

- Foreign loan words were excluded.

- All terms included had to have the same 'distribution', e.g. the same ability to combine with suffixes such as '-ish', etc.

Since the publication of their study, Berlin and Kay have been referenced in just about every study of colour naming. Many anthropologists and historians have confirmed the importance of the 'colour sequence' they identified and Berlin and Kay's later World Colour Survey more or less confirmed their results (Gage, 1999: 29). In Chapter 2 we saw, for instance, that white, black and red, Berlin and Kay's first three colours, were the only colours recognized by medieval Papal edicts and ecclesiastical writers as carrying symbolic meaning. On the other hand, Berlin and Kay also received a great deal of critique, and themselves later modified their theory to some extent after new evidence came to light, for instance the discovery that not all languages have terms for 'black' and 'white'. Berlin and Kay's critics often focused on their methodology, for instance their assumption that colour terms would always have to be single lexical items, adjectives such as 'red' or 'green'. The Hopi example has already shown that what in one language might be expressed by a noun, might, in another, be expressed by a verb or an adverb, and some languages are much more 'agglutinative' than others, that is, they make most words by adding prefixes and/or suffixes to a rather limited vocabulary of stems, rather than having a large number of separate words (see e.g. Lucy, 1997; Heeschen, 2006). Second, the use of Californian 'native speakers' could have biased the results, as they would all be bilingual and bicultural – in many cultures people only get to see more than a handful of colours on ceremonial occasions. Third, the elimination of terms that are restricted to limited domains and terms that do not also designate objects, rules out 95 per cent of the world's expressions for colour and most of the world's colour categories (Shweder and Bourne, 1984: 60). In many languages the most important colour names are derived from objects. In the Tariana language of Brazil (Wierzbicka, 1996: 331), *irite*, 'red', comes from *iri*, 'blood', and *kesolite*, 'muddy, dirty brown', from *kesole*, 'mud', while words for black, yellow, green and blue and white do not have such a derivation. On Murray Island (Australia) *mammam*, 'red', comes from *mam*, 'blood', and *bambam*, 'orange, yellow' from *bam*, 'turmeric', while *pipi*, 'grey', comes from *pi* 'ashes', for instance. Even in European languages some words (e.g. 'orange') denote both objects and colours, and where they do not, it could be that people no longer remember what they originally referred to. The elimination of loan words, finally, raises the question how languages can evolve if not as a result of cultural contact and migration, and cultural contact usually involves the adoption of foreign loan words. The Malay word for brown is *tjokolat*, the Bahasa Indonesian one *tjoklat*, from the English and Dutch words for 'chocolate', for instance, and the Battas on Sumatra have *balau* for 'blue', a word borrowed from the Dutch *blauw*.

Other critics have come up with counter-examples. The already mentioned Tariana language of Brazil, for instance, has the following colour names: *kadite* ('black'), *irite* ('red, orange, dark yellow'), *ewite*, 'yellow', *hipolite*, 'green, blue', *halite*, 'white, light, transparent' and *kesolite*, 'muddy, dirty brownish'. According to Berlin and Kay's sequence, 'brown' would have to be eliminated from this sequence, as it comes after 'blue' for which there is no separate word in Tariana. But the most trenchant critique is that Berlin and Kay's method is Anglocentric and misrepresents non-Western ways of naming colour by imposing a Western model on them. By asking people to match words with areas on a Western, scientifically constructed colour chart, Berlin and Kay assumed that the meaning of colour words always lies in the hue of colours. We have already seen that this is not necessarily the case in non-Western colour-naming systems. As Van Brakel writes (quoted by Wierzbicka, 1996: 287):

In Western languages . . . there is a bias towards hue at the expense of brightness and saturation. In other cultures, the hue aspect of colour may, as it were, be subsumed under different categories, so that it isn't really present as a separate domain.

Second, Berlin and Kay assumed that the meaning of colour names is referential, and consists of mapping names on actual colours, rather than on the conceptual meanings colour names carry in real languages:

Fixation on the spectrum colours and on physical and neurological explanations for colour perception obscures the fact that many colours of cultural interest to human beings, such as the variety of browns and tans, while now understandable as complex mixtures of light of different wavelengths, etc., are not present as distinct components of the solar spectrum.

(Hewes, quoted in Wierzbicka, 1996: 328)

Finally, they decontextualized colour, separating colour from the cultural and contextual matrix which determines people's *interest* in specific colours and leads them to name them in specific ways. In the next section we will look at two of these issues in more detail – the dominance of hue in colour naming, and the role of cultural experience in colour naming.

4.3 Colour and culture

Why could Homer use the same colour word, *leukos*, for the colour of snow, water, metallic surfaces and the sun? Not because they are all white, but because they are all reflective, shiny or luminescent. Why could he use the same word, *chloron*, for yellow as well as green things? Not because the Greeks of his time could not see the difference between these two colours, but because the things he called *chloron* (leaves, honey, sand, etc.) were all pale in colour, light and somewhat desaturated. In Homer's time, lustre, luminescence, saturation and value were somehow more important, more fundamental for the characterization of colour than hue, difficult as that might be to understand today, when hue is used as a key classifier of objects.

In the Middle Ages it was no different. Even though St Peter was supposed to be recognizable by his blue tunic and yellow cloak, in the mosaics in Venice the colour of his cloak varies from brownish grey to pale green and yellow ochre, and that of his tunic from blue to purple. Elsewhere he wears pale green over blue as well as dull brown over pale green (Gage, 1999: 71). Medieval writers might have stipulated the colours of the Trinity as blue for the Father, red for the Son, and yellow for the Holy Spirit, but even in a single twelfth-century manuscript Christ could now be red, now blue (*ibid*.: 68):

> When we think about colour, we think in the first instance of hue: we discriminate colours by their redness, blueness, etc. [In the Middle Ages], this hue-based conception had not yet developed; colours were chiefly recognized as degrees on a scale of brightness, for their position between white and black, or light and dark.

As a result, medieval colours were *families* of colours that had more or less the same value but differed in hue.

Ethnographic studies also show that hue is not always the most important aspect of colour. In Tiv, a language of Nigeria, *ii* refers to green, and to darker blues and greys, *pupu* to very light blues and light greys, and *nyian* to brown as well as to a range of warm colours, from red to yellow (see Berlin and Kay, 1991: 25). Clearly, the words *ii* and *pupu* define colour on the basis of *value*, of dark and light, and the word *nyian* defines it in terms of colour temperature. For the Tiv, light and dark, and warm and cold are not varieties or modifications of basic hues, it seems, but, instead, green, blue and grey are varieties or modifications of dark and light, and of warm and cold. Where we have a 'light blue' or a 'warm yellow', they might have a 'red dark', or a yellow warm', so to speak. In Dani, a Papuan language, even deep dark reds are co-categorized with light colours, because both are warm (see Wierzbicka, 1996: 318). And in Gu-jingarliya, an Australian Aboriginal language, red is co-classified with very light colours for a different reason – its luminosity and lustre. Native Gu-jingarliya speakers explain that reflective foil is the best example of 'red', and apply the word for 'red' to a number of very light colours. Why? Because they are all shiny, glistening and bright (*ibid*.). Again, the Tzotzil-speaking Mayan weavers in Mexico distinguish colours not just on the basis of hue and value, but also on the basis of 'discreteness', 'opacity' and 'texture' (MacKeigan and Muth, 2006: 27). And as we have already seen, Hanuhóo colour words are based on tactile, textural experience – 'wet' vs 'dry' (Conklin, 1964). Old Irish (Lazar-Meyn, 2006) even has three sets of colour words, one based on hue, one on saturation and brightness, and one on 'contextually restricted' uses. There are, for instance, three different words for 'white'. *Bán* is 'white' as we would understand it, *gel* is 'dazzling white', and *lachtna* is 'milk-coloured'. All three can be freely applied to different objects. The approach of Berlin and Kay uses hue as the single defining quality of colour. But, as we discussed in the previous chapter, colour has a range of dimensions, not just value and saturation, but also luminosity and luminescence, lustre, transparency and temperature – even aspects of texture such as roughness or smoothness, or wetness and dryness, can directly influence the way colours are understood and named.

Not only is colour naming based on a range of visible dimensions of colour, it also relates to people's experience of the natural and cultural world in which they live. We already saw how in antiquity, and throughout the Middle Ages, colours were related to the elemental aspects of the natural world: earth, air, fire and water. But the same colours were not always related to the same elements. Empedocles, in the fifth century BC, related black to water and white to fire. The writer known as the Peripatetic related white to air, water and earth and gold to fire. In the Chinese tradition, black related to water and white to metal.

Modern writers relate colour to experience in different ways. Wierzbicka, like Berlin and Kay, regards black and white as universal colours, but she gives this a different interpretation. It is not so much the *colours* black and white that are universal, it is the experience of dark and light, of day and night, and this is the reason why the words we translate as 'black' and 'white' include so many colours we would, today, not call 'black' or 'white' (Wierzbicka, 1996: 287):

> It is not true that, as has often been claimed, all languages have words for black and white . . . if a word is used to describe not only black, but also brown, grey, or dark-blue objects, then it cannot possibly mean 'black'.

In most cultures, Wierzbicka suggests, people do not classify and name colours so much as their visual experience generally: 'All languages have a word for 'see', but not all languages have a word for colour' (*ibid*.). Another fundamental aspect of colour naming, according to Wierzbicka, is people's ability to draw analogies, to see the colour of one object as *like* that of another. In colour names based on analogy, the object that gave the colour its name remains part of the meaning. Aboriginal people, for instance, do not 'abstract the colour white as a separate property of a variety of natural phenomena'. As we have seen, colour names of this kind do not count as colour names in Berlin and Kay's theory, yet they appear to be universal.

If the name of an object is to become a colour name, says Wierzbicka, that object must be a 'thing of extraordinary visual interest, a thing that dominates people's view (like the sky, the sun, the sea, or a white snowy landscape)' (*ibid*.: 315). Earth, for example, might have a different colour in different areas, but it will always have a primary importance in people's lives, and it will therefore always be a source of colour names (even today we still have *umber*, *ochre*, *terre verte*, and so on). Although colour names based on words for earth might not themselves be universal, the importance of earth as a source of colour names is (*ibid*.: 332):

'Colours as such cannot function as cognitive anchors for colour naming. It is the shared concepts of fire, sun, sky, vegetation and so on which function as cognitive anchors for colour naming.'

Colour names, therefore, start their life as metaphors. The word 'metaphor' comes from the Greek, meaning, simply, 'transport'. Metaphor therefore implies the idea of 'transfer', of transferring something from one place to another, on the basis of a perceived similarity between the two 'places', e.g. transferring the word 'wave' from the environment of water to the environment of light on the basis of a perceived similarity, a partial analogy, its periodicity. Lakoff and Johnson (1980: 211) see metaphor as 'one of the most basic mechanisms we have for understanding experience', not only among native peoples, but also today, and also in science (for instance, the idea of 'light wave'). Most metaphors might once have embodied new ideas, new insights, but are no longer experienced as metaphors. They embody our everyday normality. They are the 'metaphors we live by'. A key idea in their theory of metaphor is that we understand metaphors on the basis of our concrete experience: 'No metaphor can ever be comprehended or even adequately represented independently of its experiential basis' (*ibid.*: 19). Such experiences might be *physical experiences* shared by all human beings, such as walking upright, or night and day. They might also be *physical interactions with our environment* – moving things, manipulating things and so on, so that, for instance, the concrete action of 'building' can become a metaphor for the much more abstract concept of 'theory', allowing us to say things like '*support* your theory with *solid* facts' or 'we have a *framework* for understanding'. And they might also be *interactions with people*, as when we compare diseases with military operations (e.g. 'malignant tumours invade even when they grow slowly', 'rogue cells will eventually regroup and mount a new assault on the organism' – the examples come from Sontag (1979: 64–5). Colour words, too, can be understood on this basis. The Hanuhóo word *latuy*, 'green', transfers the quality of 'greenness' from wet, juicy plants to other objects, just as 'light wave' transfers the quality of periodicity from waves of water to other 'waves'.

Clearly the ideas of Wierzbicka, and of Lakoff and Johnson, acknowledge both universal and culturally specific human experiences. However, like other writers on colour names, Wierzbicka's examples are mostly from small languages. For the purposes of social semiotics we cannot restrict ourselves to the experiences of nature, animal husbandry, agriculture which she and other ethnographers have documented and which have dominated the literature on colour names. In modern urban life, the experience of nature has become less direct, more mediated and more symbolic. Nature might no longer be a 'thing of extraordinary visual interest' that 'dominates people's view' in everyday life – in big cities even the experience of light and dark has changed significantly. Contemporary colour naming is as complex and varied as ever, and certainly not restricted to the 11 basic colour terms of Berlin and Kay. Lipstick names, for instance, (*Prune Drama Girl*, *Daring Rose*, *Wicked Brown*, *Pink in the Limo*, *Roach*, *Cheese-curl-fingers-orange*) do not always indicate the actual colour of the lipstick, and Lancôme, like the Gu-jingarliya of Australia, foregrounds the luminosity and lustre rather than the hues of their lipsticks: 'Incredibly luminous, vibrant colour. . . . Light-maximizing pigments™ use light as a prism to bring you the most intense, lasting shine' (Lancôme, 2010).

4.4 Colour naming today

Today, colours are not only named, but also numbered. A bewildering range of 'colorimetric' methods have developed to do so. I already discussed two of the most well-known methods in Chapter 3, the Munsell system (the version used by Berlin and Kay identifies 320 colours) and the Pantone Matching System (which can identify 747 colours). The number of colours these systems can identify gradually expanded. The Acoat Colour Codification system, for instance, developed in 1978 by Sikkens, a Dutch paint manufacturer, can identify about a million colours (Fischer, 1996: 210), still a long way from the 10,000,000 colours the human eye can apparently distinguish (Stiles and Wyszecki, 2000).

Colour measurement is important for companies that develop and market colours and colourful objects. Imperial Chemical Industries (ICI), for instance, identifies its Vibrant Jade Cluster 1 (a saturated dark green) as Dulux 421GG 08/250 and the Groupe Carli in Paris uses the 'Pantone Textile System' to protect the colours of their brand with designations like 13-0850 TP (*soleil*) and 17-1525 TP (*terre rouge*), etc. (see Wyler, 2006: 116). In a booklet called *HSBC Brand Basic Elements* (HSBC, 2006), HSBC prescribes the exact HSBC colours so as to guarantee 'the integrity of [HSBC's] trademark corporate signature':

> HSBC red can be achieved using PANTONE™1795 red. Four colour halftone reproduction can achieve an acceptable match to HSBC red (Cyan 0%, Magenta 94%, Yellow 100%, Black 0%. HSBC grey is the Group's secondary corporate colour and can be achieved using PANTONE™ 423 grey. For halftone reproduction a 44% tint of black can achieve an acceptable match to HSBC grey.

Mercedes-Benz went further and developed its own silver paint (Mercedes-Benz, 2010):

> Mercedes-Benz, together with BASF, has developed a new paint that is called Alubeam. The new Mercedes-Benz CL 65 AMG will be the first to wear it. Chrome, polished silver, its mirror-like shine can't be missed . . . Each car is painstakingly coated with extra reduced paint that contains super-small aluminium flakes. The flakes in the standard metallic paint measure from 100 to 300 nanometer and the special paint has flakes that measure from 30 to 50 nanometer. It's like spraying liquid metal.

And Coca-Cola is so confident of the uniqueness of its 'Coca-Cola Red' that it makes it freely available (Coca-Cola, 2010):

> There is no longer a PMS colour match number for Coca-Cola Red. All major paint stores should have Coca-Cola Red computerized. You may simply ask for 'Coca-Cola Red' or perhaps take a colour sample with you to the paint store.

But colorimetric systems have not replaced colour names. Paint manufacturers and the manufacturers of fabrics, beauty products, and so on, not only invent (or resurrect) an ever larger number of colours, they also constantly add new colour names. A single paint manufacturer might have some 1,500 names on the books (Wyler, 2006: 117), and these names are just as much motivated by the dominant 'interests' of modern urban life as the colour names of the Hanuhóo or the Ovahero were by their interests in plants and cattle. In a study of the colour names in fashion magazines such as *Vogue* and *Marie Louise*, Wyler (2006) found that, although the basic colour names *were* used, together with colour names that are specific for fabrics, such as *khaki* and *navy blue*, the majority of colour names also designated objects, for instance food and plants (*cherry, herb, lemon, lime, sage, wisteria*) and inorganic objects and landscape features (*amethyst, coral, horizon, mist, ocean, sea, sky, stone, forest, Sahara*). Most colour names were not 'mono-lexemic' but modified to indicate value or saturation (*light grey*, *soft blue*, *deep brown*), and/or context (*desert khaki*, *admiral blue*, *midnight navy*, *dark lagoon blue*, *dark mineral sage*, *light antique indigo*). As we have seen, critics of Berlin and Kay have accused them of Anglocentrism, of imposing 'Western' interpretations of colour on the colour-naming systems of other cultures. But looking a little further than the colour wheels of the textbooks, we can see that 'Western' colour names are not all that different from those of other cultures. They are just as motivated by interest as the systems of traditional cultures. It is just that the 'things of extraordinary interest' and the 'things that dominate people's view' in everyday urban life are rather different. Rather than the green of fresh bamboo, we have the '*daring rose*' of constant sexual titillation; the *lagoon blue* of romantic holidays; the faded prestige of things antique; the eye-catching red of Coca-Cola and HSBC. And nuances matter. We notice the subtle differences between the silver of different brands of car or the reds of different trademarks. As Gage has said (1999: 107):

> In everyday life, we are, I suggest, far more concerned with nuances than with the saturated 'primary' colours whose identification has been relatively recent, and whose importance has largely been confined to the specialized contexts of the painter's workshop and the physical or psychological laboratory.

A closer look at one example will help develop this idea a little further. A Dulux catalogue of white interior paints first introduces the meanings of 'whites and neutrals' – they can be 'cool', 'neutral' or 'warm'. The meaning of 'cool' white comes from its temperature ('cool', 'refreshing') and from its lightness 'light', qualities which, the catalogue suggests, convey 'peace and tranquillity':

> Cool whites bring refreshing light to both classic and contemporary interiors to create a mood of peace and tranquillity.

'Warm' whites, or rather creams, again gain their meaning from colour temperature ('warmth') and are both 'luxurious' and 'welcoming':

> Luxurious creams coordinate beautifully with polished wood and textured soft furnishings to create a sense of warmth and welcome.

'Neutrals' are much like 'cool whites' but without reference to colour temperature:

> Sophisticated and subtle, neutral whites pick up accents of natural light to bring a sense of serenity and space to living and dining areas.

The names of these whites are almost always modified to suggest subtle nuances, but in only two cases is there a hint of value, of darker and lighter variants (*Off White* and *White on White*). As in the Middle Ages, many of the colour names refer to the materiality of the colours, to the substances from which they are, supposedly, made: *Bone White*, *Shell White*, *White Opal*, *Pearl White*, *Chalk USA*, *Magnolia*, *Lamarque* (Lamarque is a white rose), *Raw Cotton*, and *Clotted Cream*. Other names create associations with specific objects: *Napkin White*, *Cottontail White*, *Crewelwork*, *Hog Bristle* and *Peplum White* (a peplum is an overskirt). Interior house paints are, of course, no longer made from chalk or bone or shell, and, in any case, only paint manufacturers and artists are likely to be aware of the way in which specific

Where we are now

We've been talking with many of you to understand where we are now, and what it's like working here and what could be better. Our research shows that many of you enjoy working for Rank Xerox and genuinely want to make it even better.

One thing we're all clear about is that we want to change. You can see from the illustration that we've become more of a yes but... company when we really need and want to be a yes and... company.

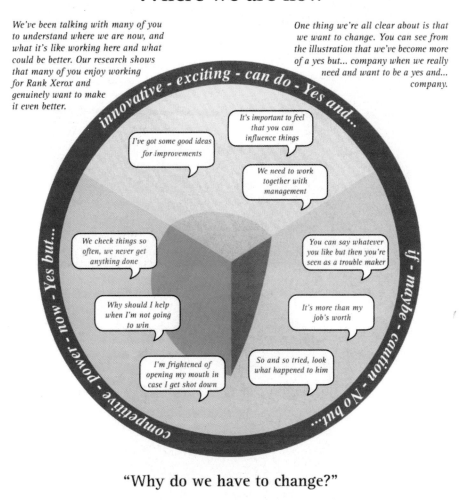

innovative - exciting - can do - Yes and...

It's important to feel that you can influence things

I've got some good ideas for improvements

We need to work together with management

We check things so often, we never get anything done

You can say whatever you like but then you're seen as a trouble maker

Why should I help when I'm not going to win

It's more than my job's worth

I'm frightened of opening my mouth in case I get shot down

So and so tried, look what happened to him

competitive - power - now - Yes but...

if - maybe - caution - No but...

"Why do we have to change?"

Why do we have to change - certainly not for the sake of change! We've all recognised that the world in which we do business has changed and will continue to do so.

We need to be innovative to keep pace with our marketplace and our customers. What's good is that during our discussions with you, many of you have some good ideas on how to improve things. What we need now is for us all to take action.

1.1   Xerox report on staff satisfaction questionnaire. © Xerox, 1996.

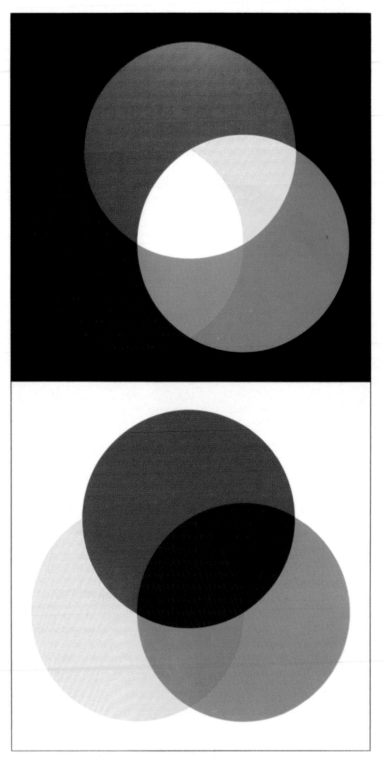

3.1   Additive and subtractive colour mixing.

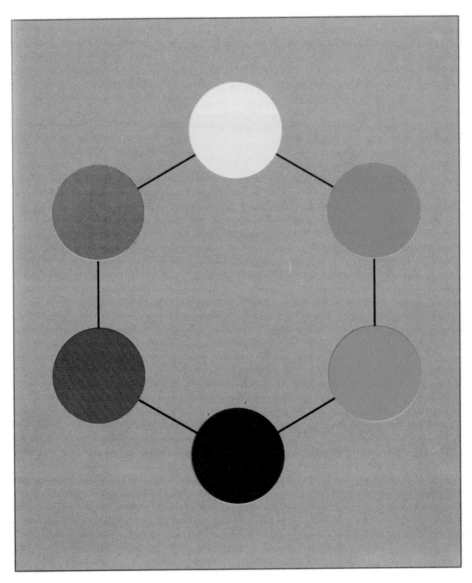

3.2   Colour wheel with primary and secondary colours.

3.3   Afterimage. Stare for 20 seconds at the green circle and then close your
       eyes. You will 'see' a red circle.

3.4   Harald Küppers' 'Colour sun' showing different values of 12 colours (Küppers, 1991: 107).

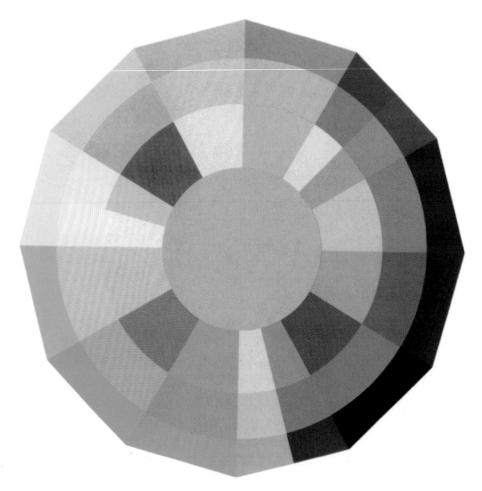

3.5   Levels of saturation, with the most saturated colours at the outer edge of the circle.

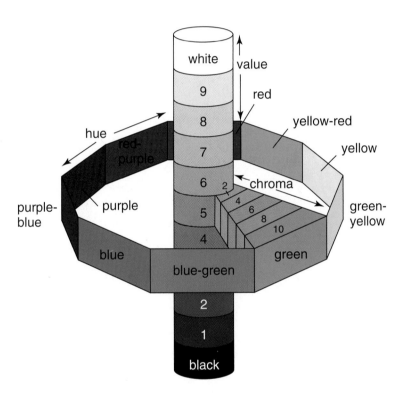

3.6   Munsell colour sphere.

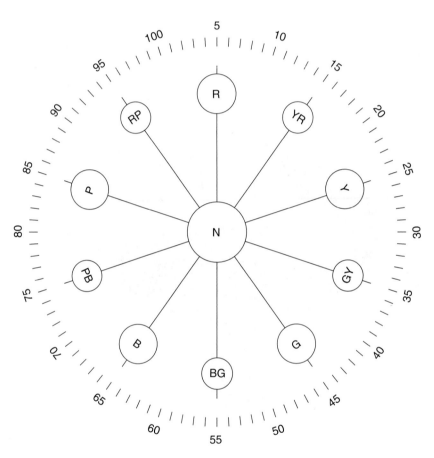

3.7   Munsell's numbering system.

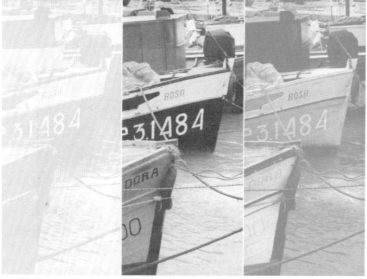

3.8
The three-colour printing process uses three plates, printing dots in yellow, magenta and cyan.

light area

highlight

form shading

form shadow

reflected shadow

cast shadow

3.9
Highlights, shading and shadow.

3.10 El Greco, *Madonna and child with Saint Martina and Saint Agnes*, from the Widener Collection. Image courtesy of the Board of Trustees, National Gallery of Art, Washington.

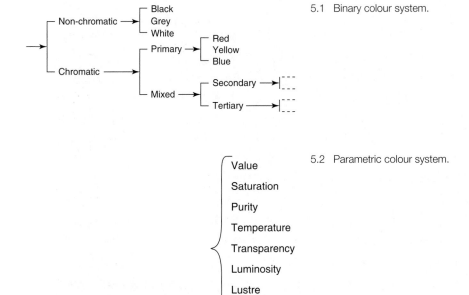

5.1 Binary colour system.

5.2 Parametric colour system.

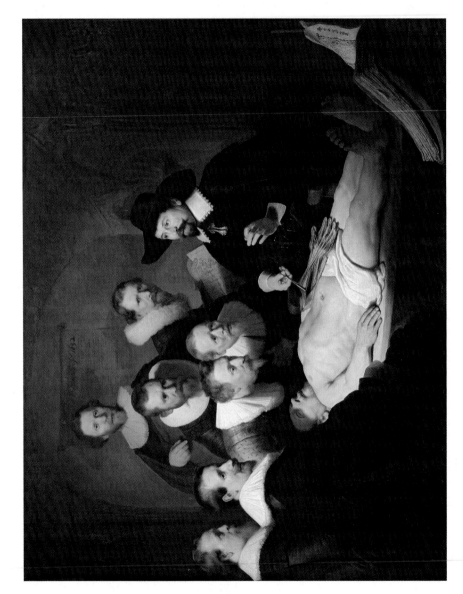

5.3   *The Anatomy Lesson of Doctor Tulp* (Rembrandt, 1632).

 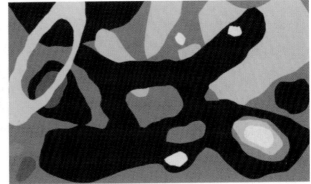

5.4   Proportional colour inventory.

 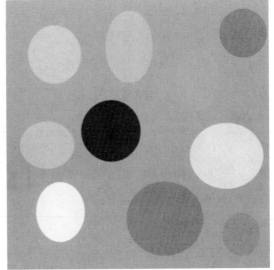

5.5   Non-proportional colour inventory.

5.6   Arrows design (Rachel Moore, 2003). rachey1982@hotmail.com

5.7 Design by Clare Perkins (2007). clareyperkins@yahoo.co.uk

6.1 Vincent van Gogh, *Le café de nuit* (The Night Café). Courtesy of Yale University Art Gallery. Bequest of Stephen Carlton Clark, B.A. 1903.

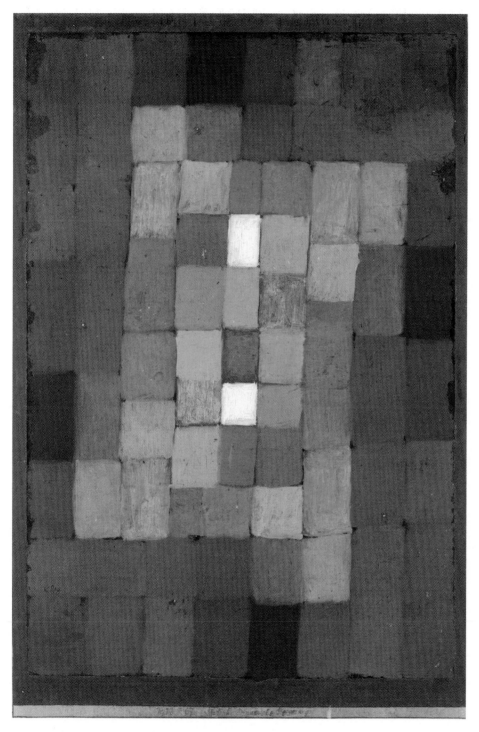

6.2   Paul Klee, *Static Dynamic Gradation* (1923). Image copyright The Metropolitan Museum of Art/Art Resource/SCALA, Florence. © Photo SCALA, Florence.

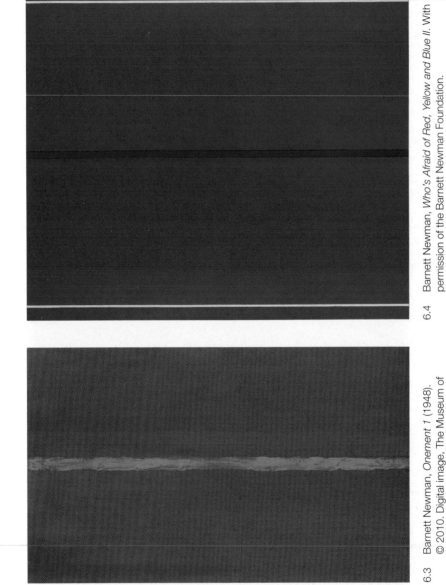

6.4   Barnett Newman, *Who's Afraid of Red, Yellow and Blue II*. With permission of the Barnett Newman Foundation.

6.3   Barnett Newman, *Onement 1* (1948). © 2010. Digital image, The Museum of Modern Art, New York/SCALA, Florence. With permission of The Barnett Newman Foundation.

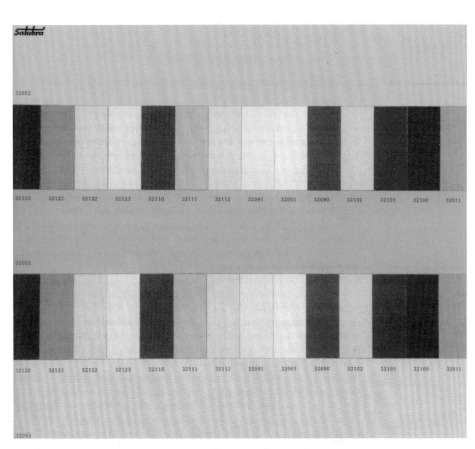

6.5   Le Corbusier, *Purist Still Life*. © ADAGP, Paris and DACS, London 2010.

6.6   Kunsthal, Rotterdam.

7.1   Historic colours (*House Beautiful*, September 1998: 21). © Colin Poole, with permission of PhotoWord Limited.

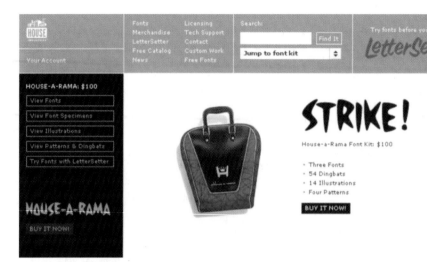

7.2   House Industries web page.

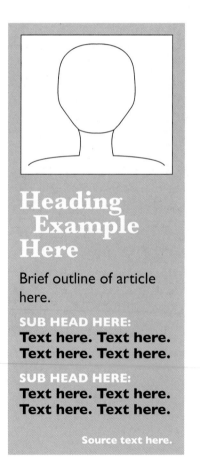

7.3   Magazine layout

TIPS FOR ASSESSING JOINT PAIN (CONTINUED)

- Clarify and record the *mechanism of injury*, particularly if there is a history of trauma.
- Determine whether the pain is *localized* or *diffuse, acute* or *chronic, inflammatory* or *noninflammatory.*

Low Back Pain. Ask "Any pains in your back?" *Back-ache* is the second most com-on reason for office visits. Ask if the pain is in the midline over the vertebrae, or off midline. If the pain radiates into the legs, ask about any associated numbness, tingling, or weakness.

See Table 16-1, Low Back Pain, pp. 301–302. Causes of *midline back pain* include vertebral collapse, disc herniation, epidural abscess, spinal cord compression, or spinal cord metastases. *Pain off the midline* in sacroiliitis, trochanteric bursitis, sciatica, or hip arthritis

Check for bladder or bowel dysfunction.

Present in *cauda equine syndrome* from S2–S4 tumor or disc herniation

Neck Pain. Ask about location, radiation into the arms, arm or leg weakness, bladder or bowel dysfunction.

Often from C7 or C6 spinal nerve compression from foraminal impingement

Joint Pain. Proceed with "Do you have any pain in your joints?"

Ask the patient to *point to the pain*. If *localized* and involving only one joint, it is *monoarticular.*

Consider trauma, monoarticular arthritis, tendonitis, or bursitis. Hip pain near the greater trochanter suggests trochanteric bursitis.

If *polyarticular*, does it migrate from joint to joint, or steadily spread from one joint to

Migratory pattern in *rheumatic fever* or *gonococcal arthritis*; progressive and symmetric in *rheumatoid arthritis*

7.4   Page from medical textbook (Bickley, 2009: 274).

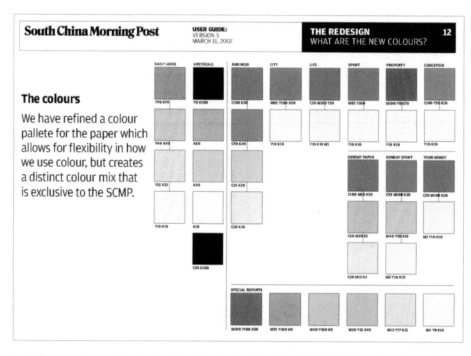

7.5   Colour scheme of the *South China Morning Post* (De Vries, 2008). Designed by de Luxe & Associates.

pigments are manufactured. Most people would not know, for instance, that Spanish White is 'an impalpable power prepared from chalk and used as a white pigment'. Perhaps it is not the precise reference that matters, but the sense of exclusivity and expensiveness (e.g. *opal* and *pearl*) that is important, and the sense that these paints are 'natural' when in fact they are cheap and mass produced. The use of place names suggests the quality of specially imported or handmade paints (*Spanish White*, *China White*, *Berkshire White*, *Stowe White*), just as with 'ultramarine' in the Middle Ages. Where objects lend their name to the colours it is, again, not the objects that matter, but the values with which they are associated – the cleanliness of starched white napkins; the fluffiness of the white rabbit's tail. Again, in some cases most consumers might not get the reference. *Crewelwork*, for instance, is 'embroidery in which a design is worked in worsted on a background of linen or cotton' (OED), and a *Peplum* is 'a kind of overskirt, 1863', (OED). Other modifiers convey such values more directly, for instance *Natural White* and *Antique White USA*. And names like *Gentle Touch* and *Whisper White* suggest the 'peace' and 'tranquillity' the catalogue associates with white.

Values of this kind matter to the modern consumer. They create identity. They position the home owner as someone who values peace and tranquillity, or, if orange or red is chosen, excitement and passion (*Sultry Glance*, *Sheer Passion*, *Bright Delight*). Such values inform Dulux paints not only in their catalogue, but also in everyday life, as in this quote from the Internet (Completecraft, 2010):

> Dulux Stowe White is Karen's favourite colour and has been used extensively throughout her house . . . 'I love the simplicity of white as it is clear and calm and can be mixed with anything to create a different look', states Karen.

In the same way that Mercedes-Benz foregrounded the metallic texture of its silver paint ('It's like spraying liquid metal'), Dulux foregrounds the materialities of its colours by blurring the boundaries between colour and texture, between the visual and the tactile:

> Popularity in textures continues to grow as they add . . . tactile, contemporary elements to rooms. *Suede* [creates] a stylish finish for feature walls or throughout the room which echoes the look of suede. *Metallic* creates the subtle polished sheen of precious metals on your walls, doors, trim or furniture. *River Rock* [is] a subtle texture inspired by weathered rocks from nature's river beds that adds a natural ambience to your room. And *Pearlustre* [is] an intriguing and luxurious lustre which adds vibrancy and radiance to your home.

As we have seen, colour-name researchers have gradually discovered that the colour-naming systems of past cultures and traditional cultures are not necessarily based on hue, and might instead be based on luminosity, lustre, texture, and so on. Dulux made the same discovery in its own way. In its naming of colours, it reintroduced the materialities and histories of paint, albeit only on a symbolic level. It is time we do the same thing in colour theory, and that is what I will attempt in the next chapter.

Exercises

1 According to Terri MacKeigan and Stephen Muth (2006), Tzotzil weavers use two types of colour words. Which are they? What is the function of each? And how does each relate to, on the one hand, Berlin and Kay's theory of basic colour terms, and, on the other hand, the idea of 'experiential metaphor' explained in this chapter?

We found a high level of variation across speakers. For example, speakers in San Andrés who used terms deriving from *ik'* ('black') or *sak* ('white') to describe grey had never heard the word *chak-xik* (from a brown cloth no longer used) which is used for 'grey' in the neighbouring hamlet of Chamula. In these communities, where there is little of the kind of standardization brought by Western literacy, individuals do not defer to any other as an authority for what a colour 'should' be named. They name colours in a more flexible manner, according to how they want to express themselves at a particular time and place and indexically referring to the seasonal cycles of plants, the sky, and the mountain valleys which they share with all Tzotzil speakers. . . .

The contemporary language of colour in Tzotzil has roots in pre-Conquest Mayan beliefs. The central concept of life was framed by belief in a square or quadrilineal universe in which the cardinal directions were represented by a deity and his/her corresponding cosmological cycle, number and colour: white (north), yellow (south), red (east), black (west) and with blue-green for the centre of the earth . . .

It seems that old beliefs still constrain some of the conventions for the use of colour words in Tzotzil, determining which words are used more frequently, restricting the number of root terms and encouraging the maintenance of a large number of modifiers to further qualify the basic colours. . . .

Tzotzil weavers often referred to the landscape when trying to recall terms, holding up chips to match colours with the environment. The names of landscape features were often used: *yaxal vinajel* 'blue-green of the sky', *yaxal-balamil* 'blue-green of fields', *yaxal vits* 'blue-green of a distant hill', *yaxal yanal nichim* 'blue-green of the leaves on a flower stem'. In these constructions, the use of the root *yax* 'blue-green' is very general and has a large footprint in the colour space, but the extensive use of modifiers allows for high specificity. The memory-load of such a large colour vocabulary can be somewhat relieved by easy reference to a constant and shared landscape. Support from this interpretation comes from the fact that Tzotzil has been classified as having only five basic terms . . . despite having such a large colour lexicon, and also from the fact that the blue-green category has not split, despite the addition of pink, orange, brown and purple categories as long as three decades ago. This evolution sequence differs from the Berlin and Kay model and may have been influenced by long-standing Mayan speech practices.

2 Find the colour chart of a brand of lipstick and analyse the values that the names of the colours suggest.

3 Photograph a multi-coloured subject (e.g. the mosses on a stone, autumn leaves, the discolorations caused by rust). Invent names for the colours, to be used in a catalogue for interior house paints, and explain what values the colours might suggest in this context.

5 A Parametric Theory of Colour

5.1 Colour meaning

For some time now, the dominant approach to colour meaning has been psychological, and psychology has universal pretensions, however much these might, at times, be qualified by a mention of cultural and other differences. As we have discussed in Chapter 2, contemporary applied colour psychology understands colour meaning as near-instinctive – as emotive and expressing personality, and, as 'conative', to use Jakobson's term (Jakobson, 1960: 355), as directly affecting behaviour, calming or stimulating people, a tranquilllizer or a pep pill. Yet I cannot help thinking that, today, people's colour choices are not, or no longer, 'instinctive', but tutored, conscious and explicit. Lifestyle magazines and television makeover programmes constantly 'instruct' readers and viewers in the meanings of the latest fashionable colours, albeit often in playful and tongue-in-cheek language. And their discussions of colour meaning are increasingly based on cultural and historical references rather than on affect-laden adjectives and the psychology of personality. Compare the following two quotes. In the first, colour consultant Lacy (1996: 29) describes the meaning of pink in terms of 'personality'. The second comes from a prediction of 'hot' colours for the coming season by the Color Marketing Group, an international association of 1,700 colour designers (quoted in Wyler, 2006: 125) and describes the meaning of a particular blue in terms of cultural-historical references.

> A warm pink entrance hall indicates a home which is warm and loving. People using this colour like to care for others.

> Blue Air technology melts retro Blue in this fresh breeze from the 60's classic cars.

For the moment the two approaches exist side by side. Fashion designers, for instance, sometimes talk in terms of colour preferences and colour psychology, for example Ana Šekularac (quoted in Mora, 2009: 169), in the first of the two quotes below, at other times in terms of colour schemes that are inspired by cultural-historical references, for example Davina Hawthorne (*ibid.*: 101), in the second quote:

> I have two favourite colours: black and red. . . . Red catches people's attention and evokes the strongest reaction of all colours. Red carries a largely positive connotation, being associated with courage, energy, strength and determination, loyalty and honour, as well as emotions such a happiness, passion and love.

> For my SS 2008 collection, the inspiration was a mix of armour, the floral and handcrafts. Recycled flowers were hand painted with gold and then beaded and embroidered. The collection displays a multitude of colour changing subtly from layers upon layers of dirty blue, red and orange florals to intense bright gold.

A key difference between these two approaches is that colour preferences and the personality traits they are symptomatic of, are supposedly deep-seated and hard to change, while the cultural and historical references of particular colours, on the other hand, are easier to change, because any given colour can be linked to a wide range of cultural and historical references. This facilitates reinterpreting colours, newly connecting them to themes and issues that have current cultural resonance, so as to be able to respond to fashion's demand for constant change. In this context, 'character' becomes 'lifestyle identity', a form of identity that can be changed at will (if you have the money to do so) and in which beliefs and values are expressed by preferred leisure time activities and consumer choices rather than personality traits. In Chapter 7, I will discuss this in more detail but, before I can do so, I need to develop a way of understanding colour that moves beyond hue, beyond the colour wheel and the colour spectrum, and beyond colour psychology, a way of understanding colour that takes account of the materiality of colour, and that reintegrates the material characteristics of colour with its role in contemporary cultural expression and social communication, because the traditional approach of matching individual hues to specific meanings, of saying 'red means this' and 'green means that', does not work and leads to too many contradictions.

What about yellow, for instance? For Goethe (1970: 307), yellow is 'bright, serene, gay, softly exciting', 'warm' and 'agreeable', but liable to contamination, for example with green, which would make it 'sulphurous', or on dull surfaces which would make it 'foul' and 'ignominious' (ibid.: 308). For Kandinsky (1977: 37), 'yellow, if steadily gazed at, . . . has a disturbing influence, and reveals in the colour an insistent, aggressive character'. The well-known American colour theorist Birren (1961: 143) says that 'modern Americans' see yellow as 'cheerful, inspiring, vital, celestial' and relate it to 'high spirit' and 'health', and colour consultant Lacy describes yellow (1996: 20) as 'warm and expansive', 'activating the mind and opening it up to new ideas', although 'darker yellows can have an adverse effect and create pessimism and negativity' and 'too pale a yellow can sap energy'. What about blue? For Goethe, it 'brings a principle of darkness with it' (1970: 310) and 'gives us an impression of cold'. For Kandinsky (1977: 38), it is 'the typical heavenly colour', creating a feeling of rest, though 'when it sinks almost to black, it echoes a grief that is hardly human' and 'when it rises towards white . . . its appeal grows weaker and more distant'. Birren (1961: 43) sees blue as 'subduing, melancholy, contemplative, somber', and relates it to 'gloom, fearfulness, furtiveness', while Lacy (1996: 22–3) describes it as 'a very healing colour, soothing, calming and cooling', 'associated with loyalty, integrity and respect, responsibility and authority', although, on its own, unbalanced with something warmer, 'it can create a feeling of coldness and introspection'. Green, finally, is 'static' and 'motionless', according to Goethe: 'The beholder has neither the wish nor the power to imagine a state beyond it' (1970: 316), while for Kandinsky (1977: 37) it is 'sickly and unreal':

> In green . . . movement ceases. . . . On exhausted men this restfulness has a beneficial effect, but after a time it becomes wearisome. Pictures painted in shades of green are passive and tend to be wearisome. In the hierarchy of colours green is the 'bourgeoisie' – self-satisfied, immovable, narrow.

And while Birren (1961: 143) sees green as 'quiet, refreshing, peaceful, nascent' but also relates it to 'ghastliness, disease, terror and guilt', Lacy (1996: 21) sees it as the colour of balance and harmony', 'relaxing and restful', 'neither warm, nor cold', and bringing 'a sense of strength and stability'.

Although there are some similarities between these glosses of colour meaning, the contrasts are more striking. Yellow can be serene as well as expansive, aggressive as well as warm and cheerful. Blue can be dark and gloomy as well as restful, healing and calming. Green can be refreshing and give a sense of strength or it can be complacent, self-satisfied and narrow. Each of these meanings makes sense on its own. Blue can be the blue of the sky on a sunny day (hence 'calm' and 'healthy') or the blue of a hazy, misty, cold day (hence 'cold' and 'gloomy'). Yellow can be 'warm' and 'bright' (the sun) as well as 'sickly' (jaundice). But out of context, none of these meanings can be seen as 'the' meaning of blue and yellow. Wierzbicka (1996) is right, the 'like' principle, the principle of analogy, is universal, but *what* people will compare to *what* will differ according to the needs and interests of different cultural and situational contexts. A better approach to the meaning of colour will have to take three things into account. First, all aspects of colour need to be considered, not just hue, and not even just hue, value and saturation. Second, the perceivable, material characteristics of colour have to be interpreted for their meaning potential – that is, for their *possible* meanings, rather than their actual meanings, because the latter can only be determined in context. And third, not only the meaning potential of colours, but also the meaning potential of *colour schemes* must be considered. After all, colours rarely come to us in isolation.

5.2 A parametric approach to colour analysis

My approach here is based on earlier work, jointly undertaken with Gunther Kress (Kress and Van Leeuwen, 2002). This work was inspired by the 'distinctive feature theory' of the linguists Roman Jakobson and Morris Halle (1956). Before Jakobson and Halle, speech sounds had been thought of as the minimal units, the basic building blocks of language. Each language has, roughly, between 30 and 70 distinct speech sounds, or *phonemes*, and phonemes are thought not to have any meaning on their own. Their function is purely distinctive. They allow words to be distinguished from each other. To pronounce the [p] and the [b] by themselves, for instance, is meaningless, but they will distinguish different words from each other, for instance [pet] from [bet] or [path] from [bath]. Not every [b] sounds the same, of course. Some may be big explosions ('BANG!!') some soft murmurings ('burburburbur'). But from a linguistic point of view this makes no difference: [bath] is still [bath], however explosive or non-explosive you pronounce the [b]. Jakobson and Halle's key innovation was to divide the phonemes further, to analyse each phoneme as a bundle of distinctive features. The [b], for instance, is frontal (pronounced in the front of the mouth), bilabial (pronounced by a movement of the lips), and plosive (characterized by a sudden release of air) and voiced. The [p] has all the same characteristics, but with one difference, it is unvoiced. In this way Jakobson and Halle could characterize the speech sounds of English with just 12 distinctive features.

Kress and I, similarly, proposed to see colours, not in a unitary way, as 'red', 'yellow', 'blue' and so on, but as bundles of features. From our point of view 'red' might exist as a theoretical concept, but it does not exist as a reality. A red is always a certain kind of red. It is always red *and* dark *and* pale *and* transparent *and* warm, and so on. However, our approach differs from that of Jakobson and Halle in two ways. First, Jakobson and Halle saw their distinctive features as *binary choices*: a phoneme is either voiced or unvoiced, either frontal or back, either tense or lax, and so on. In reality, most of the contrasts they discussed are a matter of degree. It is true that consonants are either voiced, like the [b] or the [g], or unvoiced, like the [p] or the [k]. But as already indicated, 'plosiveness' is a matter of degree, a scale from a big 'bang' to a soft 'pop'. And frontality is also a matter of degree. If you touch the tip of your tongue while saying *bid*, and then move to say *part*, you can feel the tongue moving backward and the sound gradually changing from [i] to [a]. There is no specific point where the one vowel suddenly changes into the other. From a linguistic point of view this does not matter. A [p] is a [p] however plosive, and an [i] is an [i], whether it is relatively frontal or relatively 'back'. But differences of this kind *are* heard and they *are* meaningful. In the phonological system the [b] might only serve to differentiate words, but in phonetic expression (speech and other vocalizations) it might, together with the surrounding phonemes, express 'explosiveness' or 'up-front-ness'. In another context I have written more extensively about this subject (1999: 142–50). It is the same with colour. Colour *systems* – for example colour wheels and colour spheres – create discrete units (e.g. 24 distinct hues, 10 distinct values and 10 distinct saturation levels) although colour is, in fact, a spectrum in which each colour flows into the next, a greyscale from light to dark, a continuum running from pure colour to grey, and so on.

Our second point of difference with Jakobson and Halle's theory is that we do not see the distinctive features as merely distinctive. For this reason I will, from now on, call them *parameters* rather than distinctive features. Poets have long understood that the sounds of speech contribute meaning. The composer Murray Schafer, in an essay called 'When Words Sing' (1986: 180–1), evocatively suggests this:

> B Has bite. Combustive. Aggressive. The lips bang over it
> I Highest vowel. Thin, bright, pinched sound, leaving the smallest cavity in the
> mouth. Hence useful in words describing smallness: *piccolo, petit, tiny, wee.*
> L Watery, luscious, languid. Needs juice in the mouth to be spoken properly.
> Feel it drip around the tongue. Feel the saliva in 'lascivious lecher'
> O The second most frequent vowel in English. It suggests roundness and
> perfection. Consider the sound of children's singing in the dome of a
> cathedral as heard by Verlaine 'O ces voix d'enfants chantant dans le
> coupole'
> P Pip, pop, pout. Combustive, comical. Listen to the soft popping of the
> pipesmoker

The meanings of speech sounds, as Schafer discusses them, stem directly from the material characteristics of the sounds, and/or from the way they are articulated. The [b] is aggressive because 'the lips bang over it'. The [l] is 'luscious' and 'watery' because 'it drips around the tongue'. As Schafer puts it, he is 'not interested in phonetic dogma, but in colourful metaphors that unlock secrets'. It is the same with colour meaning. The meaning potential of colours and colour schemes is based on their material characteristics. The mixed or unmixed nature of colours, for instance, can express 'purity' or 'impurity', and this can unlock a range of metaphors. Concretely experienced, actual impurity, actual 'mixed-ness', can come to express abstract concepts such as 'contamination', 'hybridity', 'fusion', and so on. In Chapter 4, I already introduced this idea in relation to the metaphor theory of Lakoff and Johnson (1980). And as already discussed in Chapter 2, experiential metaphor is not only fundamental for the way meaning is made in 'media', in forms of expression that work directly in and with the materialities of the expression matter, it is also fundamental for *semiosis*, for the creation of new meanings – 'It is from metaphor that we can best get hold of something new', as Aristotle already said (1954: 1410b).

It is important to emphasize that colours have meaning *potentials* (or metaphor potentials) rather than specific meanings, and that these meaning potentials will only be narrowed down, made more specific, in specific cultural and situational contexts. The meaning potential of lightness, for instance, is just that, 'lightness'. In religious paintings this might become 'divine light', in interior decoration it might come to mean 'peacefulness' and 'tranquillity'. It is also important to recognize the difference between *meaning potential* and *affordance*. The term 'affordance' comes from the work of James Gibson on visual perception (1979). Affordances are the potential uses of a given object, stemming from the perceivable properties of the object. Because perception is selective, depending on the needs and interests of the observer, different perceivers will notice different affordances. But those that remain unnoticed continue to exist objectively, latent in the object, waiting to be discovered. The same can be said of meaning. People will derive meaning from the material qualities of an object, for example its colour, and which qualities they notice and what significance they give to them, will depend on their needs and interests, whether these are individual and contingent and/or social and cultural, shared with a community. The term *meaning potential* (a term from Halliday, 1978), on the other hand, refers to affordances that have become part of the acknowledged semiotic resources of a culture (or narrower context). Semiotic resources such as colour can, therefore, be said to have a *theoretical* meaning potential consisting of *all* their past uses and an *actual* meaning potential constituted by those past and present uses that are acknowledged and considered relevant by the users of that resource in a specific context. The idea of metaphor ties in well with the idea of affordance. To conceive of 'light waves', we must first notice the periodicity of (water) waves. But periodicity is only one of the many things that can be observed in waves. Other affordances, as yet undiscovered, might be noted in future, based on needs and interests that have not yet arisen.

Two further points need to be made. First, the principle of experiential metaphor is not the only principle for creating meaning. As I have pointed out earlier, colour meaning can also be created on the basis of provenance, of 'where a colour comes from'. We can recognize colours as military green, navy blue, royal purple, and so on, and derive their meanings from the ideas we associate with the army, the navy or royalty. And colours can also be assigned meanings *arbitrarily*, as in the case of the colour code of London Underground maps. Nevertheless, because of its power to create new meanings, the principle of experiential metaphor is particularly important, especially today, when, after a 'monochrome age', colour is acquiring new and important roles in cultural expression and social communication. Late nineteenth- and twentieth-century artists and designers began to use colour, not for purposes of naturalistic representation, but for directly representing ideas and feelings. In this, experiential metaphor was their vehicle. As I will discuss in more detail in Chapter 6, Van Gogh was one of the first to do so. In a letter to his brother Theo, he describes, for instance, how he used the meaning potential of blueness and purity to express the idea of 'infinity' (Van Gogh, 1978: 6):

> I paint infinity, a plain background of the richest, intensest blue that I can contrive, and by this simple combination of the bright head against the rich blue background, I get a mysterious effect, like a star in the depth of an azure sky.

In due course Van Gogh's blues and yellows would enter the lexicon of historical and cultural references, deriving their meaning from their provenance, their recognizability as 'Van Gogh colours', and hence perhaps from what we know about Van Gogh as a 'tortured genius', rather than from what he was trying to express. But it is always possible to do what Van Gogh himself did, to go back to the source, to reconnect with the materiality of colour, and explore the many affordances that have not yet entered into the mainstream of cultural production.

Second, 'media' are parametric systems and 'modes' are binary systems. When colour is theorized as a 'mode', 'either-or' contrasts dominate the discussion – contrast between complementaries, for instance. Any colour is either primary or not. If it is primary, it is either red, or yellow or blue. If it is not, it is either secondary or tertiary. And so on, as shown in Figure 5.1. Each bifurcation can be seen as a choice between two options, and the option at the end of each set of bifurcations fully specifies the choice made and, therefore, in theory, the meaning. Value and saturation, too, will have to be analysed in terms of distinct steps.

Parametric systems, on the other hand, are 'both-and' systems of *gradable* features. When colour is theorized as a 'medium', each colour has some value on the scale from light to dark *and* some value on the scale from fully saturated to grey *and* some value on the scale from opaque to transparent, and so on, as shown in Figure 5.2. Its meaning potential derives from all these features in their particular proportions, just as the sound of an orchestra derives from all the instruments and their particular sound levels, or the taste of a dish from all the ingredients in their particular proportions.

Modes also abstract from the materialities that will realize the choices of their systems. A 'mode' approach to colour does not take account of the medium in which a colour is realized (oil paint, water colour, 35 mm film, PowerPoint slide, etc.) and can be applied across all these media. In a 'media'-oriented approach, on the other hand, the specific qualities of the medium matter and contribute to the meaning of the whole. Finally, modes, by and large, realize the content of representations, or, in the case of objects and spaces, the functions of these objects and spaces, while media realize the compositional cohesion, identity and emotive interpretation of representations, and the symbolic and emotive resonances of objects and spaces. It is clear, therefore, that colour is sometimes best theorized as a mode, for instance in the case of colour codes, and sometimes as a medium, for instance in modern art, and in the identity-oriented uses of colour in contemporary product design, fashion design and architecture.

Below I discuss the key parameters of colour and try to evoke their meaning potential. But the words I use to do the latter should not be taken out of context and quoted as 'the' meanings of these parameters. It should always be remembered that they interact with the other parameters, and that colour rarely stands on its own. Even though some artists have explored colour as a mode of communication in its own right, and even though, to some extent, I do the same thing in this book, we normally encounter colour as the colour *of* something, and the nature of that 'something' influences and channels its interpretation.

Value

The scale of value is the grey scale, the scale from maximally light (white) to maximally dark (black). As Wierzbicka (1996) has stressed, the difference between light and dark is a fundamental experience for all people, and there is probably no culture which has not used it to express symbolic meanings and values, even though different cultures will do so in different ways. In art, value became important in the Renaissance (*chiaroscuro*), and even more so in seventeenth-century Dutch painting, as can be seen in Figure 5.3. Pastoureau (2008: 125) explained its meaning as follows:

> For many Calvinist painters, we can even speak of a true Puritanism of colour. . . . That is the case with Rembrandt, for example, who often practices a kind of colour asceticism, relying on dark tones, restrained and limited in number (to the point that he is sometimes

accused of 'monochromy', to give precedence to the powerful effects of light and resonance. From this particular palette emerges . . . an undeniable spiritual intensity.

So here, the *absence* of colour is one of the parameters, one of the material qualities of the painting. The painter voluntarily refrains from using colour, says Pastoureau, and this can unlock metaphors such as 'asceticism' and 'austerity'. Lightness itself, meanwhile, is said to have divine resonance, creating 'an undeniable spiritual intensity'.

Saturation

Saturation is the scale from the most intense, pure manifestation of a colour to 'chromatic grey', a grey with just a tinge of that colour, and ultimately to complete desaturation, achromatic grey. If colour conveys emotion, then saturation is the fullness of that emotion, and the saturation scale is a scale that runs from maximum emotive intensity to maximally subdued, maximally toned-down emotion. In context this will acquire more precise meanings and values. High saturation might be positive, exuberant, adventurous – or vulgar or garish, if you do not like it. Low saturation might be subtle and tender – or cold and repressed, brooding and moody.

Van Gogh used saturated colour to maximize the intensity of its expression, its 'passion' (quoted in Riley, 1995: 101):

I should like to paint portraits which would appear after a century to the people living then as apparitions. By which I mean I do not endeavour to achieve this by a photographic resemblance but by means of impassioned expressions, that is to say, using our . . . modern taste for colour as a means of arriving at the expression and the intensification of the character.

The Futurist 'anti-neutral dress' manifesto I quoted earlier condemned desaturated colour ('faded, fancy, semidark and humiliating shades') and called for 'exciting colours' such as 'muscular, ultra violet, ultra red, ultra turquoise, ultra green, bright yellows and vivid oranges, and rich vermilions' (quoted in Koolhaas *et al.*, 2001: 308). In the same period, fashion designer Paul Poiret not only liberated women from the corset, but also introduced bright primary colours into fashion, thereby 'disturbing the ultra-conservative retina of the bourgeoisie' (Mora, 2009: 13).

Purity

This is the scale that runs from the maximum 'purity' of undiluted colour to maximum 'hybridity' or 'mixedness'. As we have seen, the question of purity already exercised people's minds in antiquity, when mixed colours were considered inferior to unmixed ('undefiled') colours, and it was at the heart of colour theory, leading to a range of different criteria for establishing which colours were primary – some physical, some psychological, and some linguistic: colours with commonly used single names such as 'brown' and 'green' would be pure, while colours with compound names, such as 'blue-green' or 'yellow-green' would be mixed. The search for primaries never resulted in a generally accepted system and has 'proved to be remarkably inconsequential and . . . freighted with the heavy burden of ideology' (Gage, 1999: 107). Yet we do perceive colours either as irreducible or as mixing, for instance, visible 'blueish' and visible 'reddish' characteristics, and their meaning potential derives from this experience. Some might prefer purity, some hybridity. Fashion designer Karen Walker uses 'colouring book colours', because 'they're strong and there's no complexity to them – they're totally up-front' (quoted in Mora, 2009: 81). Fashion designer Bora Aksu prefers 'in between colours' (*ibid.*: 93):

> I like colours that belie description. When you see a colour but cannot label it instantly such as 'this is red or green', this draws me to it . . . The colours in between other colours are also quite attractive.

Transparency

Transparency is the scale that runs from transparent to opaque, via translucency. A colour is transparent when light can pass through it, so that things in the background can be seen behind the coloured foreground. It is translucent when the light is partially blocked, making the background hazy, or altogether indecipherable. Watercolours are transparent, showing the paper behind the colour. Glazing shows the colours behind the glaze, coloured stain the grain of the wood. Through such media colour becomes less material, light and ethereal, lying like a film over the material it covers, and the materiality of the paper, or the canvas, or the wall of a mural, becomes part of the work, transforming and transformed by the colour. Coloured glass, in the same way, both reveals and transforms what lies behind it, 'embedding colour within a translucent overlayer' (architect Shawn Mulligan in Mora, 2009: 107). Matisse used it in a fresco of dancers above the doors to a garden, so as to place the dancers 'away from the detail of what people are doing on the earth toward the ethereal areas of sky' and, again, in a fresco in Moscow (1972: 117):

> When I undertook the Moscow Dance and Music, I had decided to put colours on flat and without shading. What seemed essential to me was the surface quantity of the colours. It seemed that these colours, applied by no matter what medium, fresco, gouache, watercolour, coloured material would give the spirit of my composition. I was quite astonished, when I saw the decorations in Moscow, to see that I had, in applying my colours, played a little game with the brush in varying the thickness of the colour, so that the white of the canvas acted more or less transparently and threw off a quite precious effect of moire silk.

Luminosity

The luminosity of a colour lies in its ability to glow from within. Luminous colours are 'self-illuminating colours that place an aura around things', as designer Alessandro Mendini has put it (Koolhaas *et al.*, 2001: 243). Lighter and more strongly saturated colours are more luminous than darker and less saturated ones, and projected colour is more luminous than surface colour. In many cultures and periods, luminosity has been one of the most highly valued characteristics of colour. While Renaissance and seventeenth-century Dutch painters depicted the light falling on people and objects, as can be seen in Figure 5.3, medieval painters wanted light to radiate directly from the colours and used contrasting blues or greens to bring out the luminosity of gold paint as strongly as possible. Its quality of radiating from within suggests the meaning potential of luminosity – splendour and glamour as well as the supernatural and the divine. In a letter to his brother Theo, Van Gogh (1978: 25) explains his use of luminous colours to signify the 'eternal':

I try to paint men and women with that something of the eternal which the halo used to symbolize and which we seek to envy by the actual radiance and vibration of our colouring.

Architect Rem Koolhaas stresses both the glamour and the magic of luminosity (Koolhaas *et al.*, 2001: 12):

We have increasingly been exposed to luminous colour, as the virtual rapidly invaded our conscious experience – colour on TV, computers, movies – all potentially 'enhanced' and therefore more intense, more fantastic, more glamorous than any real colour on real surfaces. Colour, paint, coatings, in comparison became matt and dull.

Luminescence

Here colour is emitted directly by a light source, for instance a television monitor or neon lights. Its quality of emitting light is the key to its meaning potential. Light has long been seen as supernatural. Dionysus the Areopagite, described God as 'light', 'fire' and 'fountain of light' (Eco, 2002: 102):

Light derives from Good and is the image of Goodness, hence Good is celebrated with the name of Light. . . . [Goodness] illuminates all those things able to partake of it, and its light is diffused over all things while it spreads the splendour of its rays over all the visible world.

And on the occasion of the consecration of the Church of St Denis, in 1144, Abbot Suger wrote that 'the whole church would shine with the wonderful and uninterrupted light of most luminous windows'.

Today's cities shine with the immaterial glow of humanly produced radiant objects – the light emitted by neon advertising, the brightly lit skyscrapers, and the radiance of television and computer screens.

Lustre

Lustre results from the reflectiveness of coloured surfaces, from light that is reflected rather than emitted or transmitted. The key to its meaning potential is therefore again its brilliance, its ability to light up.

In the Middle Ages, lustre came from purple gowns, from the shiny tesserae of mosaics, and from the gold overlays on paintings, sculptures and other objects. Today it comes from the gloss of expensive magazines, the metallic sheen of motorcars, the shine of marble. A *Vogue Italia New Trends Report* of 1995 hailed it as follows (quoted in Koolhaas *et al.*, 2001: 273):

Lustres: midnight satin, coloured paint, pearled, mock-crocodile and Cadillac metallic effect, high-tech fabrics with an iced luminosity, magic embroideries. Plenty of deep white.

Temperature

Temperature is the scale from blue to red. In a parametric approach to colour it becomes only one of the factors constituting the complex and composite meanings of colour, and not necessarily always the most important one. Nevertheless, although 'the' meaning of red cannot be reliably established, the red end of the colour temperature scale remains associated with warmth, energy, salience, foregrounding, and the blue end with cold, calm, distance, backgrounding. The cold–warm continuum has a wide ranging meaning potential. Itten (1970) listed transparent/opaque, sedative/stimulant, rare/dense, airy/earthy, far/near, light/heavy and wet/dry. In an actual red, warmth combines with other features. An actual red might, for instance, be very warm, medium dark, highly saturated, pure and modulated, and its meaning potential will flow from all these factors as they are applied in specific contexts.

Modulation

This is the scale that runs from fully modulated colour (for example, from a blue that is richly textured with different tints and shades, as in paintings by Cézanne) to flat colour, as in comic strips, or in paintings by Matisse. It was already recognized as a feature of colour in Goethe's *Theory of Colour* (1970[1812]), and Johannes Itten (1970: 19) notes that Titian already described it, as 'one principal hue and many variant tints and shades'. He adds that variations in saturation also play a role in modulation. Modulated colour can be used for purposes of naturalistic depiction, but it might also be used as a source of meaning on its own, suggesting qualities such as 'nuanced', 'subtle', 'variegated', or, if you don't like it, 'fussy' and 'overly detailed' – Matisse used flat colours as a reaction against the 'jumpy surface' and 'disruptive vibrato' of the modulated, textured effects other painters used (1972: 143).

Flat colour can be used to show the essential colour of things ('grass is green', 'water is blue' and so on), but it might also be used as a source of meaning on its own, for its 'boldness' and 'simplicity'. Matisse saw flat colours as 'calm' and used them to escape naturalism and stress the independent expressiveness of colour. Alessandro Mendini (Koolhaas *et al.*, 2001: 238) values modulation in architecture, but thinks it should come from the influence of the environment on, in themselves, flat colours:

> As I work increasingly as an architect, I try to be careful about the relation between colour and material: in the transparency of glass, for instance, in its translucency, its being matt or lustrous or wrinkled, its systems of veining. As a rule I tend to use a flat colour, which later acquires a nuance in relation to light and shade or through the effect of curves.

I have described modulation as a quality of a single colour, but it could also be described as characterizing a type of colour scheme. A Rothko painting, for instance, might have subtly shaded reds and maroons. Are the reds and maroons single colours? Or does the painting have a colour scheme of different reds and maroons? The question becomes easier to answer if we move from trying to interpret the meaning of individual colours to interpreting the meaning of colour schemes, as I will advocate in the next section of this chapter.

Modulation is also closely related to texture. Its use might be motivated by naturalistic considerations, such as the shape and depth of shadows, but modulations might also be distributed randomly, or display more abstract patterns – striations, mottling, veining, and so on – which can themselves be given interpretations, on the basis of *their* 'distinctive features' – their straightness or roundness, their horizontal or vertical or circular orientation, their regularity or irregularity – these qualities too can 'unlock metaphors' (see Djonov and Van Leeuwen, in press).

Differentiation

Differentiation, too, is a property of colour schemes. It is the scale that runs from mono-chrome to the use of a maximally varied palette. Its meaning potential again flows from what it is. High differentiation can mean 'diversity' or 'exuberance', low differentiation 'restraint'. In an article from a home decoration magazine which I will discuss in more detail in Chapter 7, a couple 'uses nearly the whole spectrum in their house' and comment that 'it's great that there are so many bright shades in the house. It's a shame people aren't more adventurous, It's when you start being timid that things go wrong' (*House Beautiful*, September 1998: 21). High differentiation here means 'adventurousness', and low differentiation 'timidity', but it is clear that in another context restraint might have a more positive value.

It might seem difficult to tell the difference between modulation and differentiation, but in considering actual examples it is usually reasonably easy to tell the two apart. In Figure 5.7, for instance, the overall differentiation is low, white, pale blues, slightly deeper blues and violet. There are therefore three different colours, white, blue and violet, and each is modulated – varying in value, degree of transparency, and patterns of striation.

5.3 Colour schemes

Colours rarely come separately. Even the 'little black dress' combines with the tones of the skin and the hair of its wearer; even the colour field painting hangs on a white wall. Artists and theorists alike have always seen colours as interactive, brightening or dulling each other, harmonizing or clashing. In a letter to his brother Theo, Van Gogh (1978: 28), explained how he had expressed 'the terrible passions of humanity' by means of 'a clash and contrast of the most disparate reds and greens'. Matisse advocated designing a scheme of three to six colours before starting a painting 'to find the equations that make up the life of a picture'. As he explained this to his students (1995: 267), while pointing at a house: 'Do you see the colour of the foundation, of the molding, of the wall and the shutters? That forms a unity, a similar unity to that which a picture needs.'

There are colour schemes that mark an era, a culture, or an institution. The traditional Indian colour scheme is marked by red-orange, yellow-orange, rust colour, as well as blue-purple, blue-green and yellow-green. The traditional Japanese scheme has more blues, purples and greys, as well as browns and red-orange colours. Armies might have olive greens and khaki, or, today, the earth colours of camouflage patterns. The Mondrian colour scheme of pure red, yellow and blue (plus black and white) came to characterize Modernity, while a colour scheme of pale, anaemic cyans and mauves became, for a time, a key signifier of Postmodernity. Then there are the arbitrary colour schemes which use distinct, strong colours, red for fire protection devices, blue for switch control boxes, green for first aid equipment and medicines, and so on, and the individual palettes of artists or designers, such as fashion designer Bora Aksu (Mora, 2009: 93):

I love the effect of splashing outstanding colours into a muted colour palette. My AW 2007–2008 collection was a collection of warm eggplants and fuchsias with contrasting silver grey.

In Chapter 3, I discussed some of the ideas on colour schemes in the colour theory literature. To a large degree these were defined by the colour wheel. Here I will try to extend this by including all the parameters I have discussed in the previous section. All can contribute to the meaning potentials of colour schemes, although some will be more dominant than others, and although differentiation will always be a particularly important feature.

Colour schemes (or parts of colour schemes) might also be inspired by cultural or natural references, and derive their meanings from provenance. Le Corbusier saw ocean liners and aeroplanes as the ultimate of functionality. But in the Le Corbusier Centre in Zürich he used colour to *symbolize* the functional virtues of ocean liners, to make the building *look* like an ocean liner by using the grey steel of battleships and the red, yellow and blue of semaphore flags (Riley, 1995: 212). Many contemporary designers use colour in this way, referring to the cultural and historical meanings of an entire scheme, or even of several schemes, combining in a 'composite of connotations', as with Bora Aksu whose designs use 'a pinch of punk, a pinch of Edwardian and a pinch of dream' while at the same time taking inspiration from 'nomadic warriors' (see Mora, 2009: 93).

Contemporary designers like Aksu think semiotically about colour, rather than in terms of the colour wheel harmonies and contrasts that still dominate the textbooks. Here is another example, from fashion designer Martin Lamothe (*ibid.*: 33):

The colour mustard is simultaneously warm and masculine, earthy and ordinary as well as being difficult and conceptual. Consequently it's the intelligent alternative to brown and it combines with the palette of colours that appeals to me: pinks, mints, greys.

Although the idea of 'colour harmony' has dominated discussion of colour schemes in the literature, colours not only harmonize, they can also contrast, and the nature of this contrast can play a key role in the meaning potential of the scheme, whether it is used for naturalistic purposes or otherwise. Monet enhanced the orange glow of the sun reflected in water by surrounding it with duller, darker colours. Van Gogh expressed 'the terrible passions of humanity' by means of clashing reds and greens. And modern designers like clashes too. Fashion designer Easton Pearson 'loves to highlight intense colours against a base of the neutral ones of the earth' (*ibid.*: 149), and fashion designer Allegra Hicks 'teams saturated colours with muted organic ones', combining 'these intense colours with chic earthy tones to bring a sophisticated, modern feeling to my collection of print' (*ibid.*: 127).

The *proportionality* of the different colours in a scheme is fundamental. A colour in a colour scheme might be 'anomalous', contrasting with the others, so that a small touch of it might create a strong accent. This is often done to draw special attention to something, to make something salient, whether through a contrast in value (the eye is the most salient element in a face because of the strong contrast between the dark pupil and the white of the eye), a contrast in hue (e.g. a red amid paler colours), a contrast in saturation, or some other contrast. The architect Norman Foster, for instance, uses neutral colours in his designs for airports and metro stations, to 'offer some calm, tranquility and reassurance' amid the 'stresses of twentieth century travel', but strong colours, for example reds, for direction signs and announcements. But 'accents' of this kind might also add a touch of excitement to an otherwise placid, calm scheme, as in the case of Bora Aksu who 'loves the effect of splashing outstanding colours into a muted colour palette' (quoted in Mora, 2009: 93).

There is interest both in analysing ready-made colour schemes, for instance the colour charts of paint manufacturers, and in extracting, and then analysing, colour schemes from pictures and other visual designs. Hornung (2005: 114ff.) suggests reconstructing the colour schemes of pictures by matching their colours to those of a set of coloured strips of paper, and then collating these strips either in a 'proportional colour inventory' which roughly indicates proportionality (see Figure 5.4), or in a 'non-proportional colour inventory', if this proves impossible (Figure 5.5). Making such an inventory is an excellent way of learning to 'see' colours and the way they combine.

When it comes to interpreting colour schemes, not all parameters will play an equally important role, and we need to single out the aspects that most clearly define the colour scheme or 'palette', starting with overall characteristics, and then moving to contrasts. Figure 5.6 shows a pattern design by Rachel Moore. It contains propeller-like shapes (or machine-like flowers?) against a background of downwards pointing yellow verticals.

- All the colours in the scheme are unmodulated. Each makes a strong, 'undiluted' statement. There is no room for nuances here, with one small exception, the shading between the white and the pink on some of the 'blades' of the propeller (or petals of the flower?).

- The colours are quite saturated and, with the exception of the black, relatively light and luminous, especially the yellow, set off as it is against the blue. Clearly, this design has a certain intensity, a certain upbeat brightness.

- There are six colours in the scheme – blue, yellow, pink, white, grey and black. There is strong, bold differentiation between the white, the grey and the black, between the blue and the yellow, and between these two primary colours and the pink.

- It would be relatively 'naturalistic' to depict a machine part in grey, white and black, but the pink is unusual. This entitles us to interpret it symbolically, as a symbol of femininity. On the other hand, if we interpret the shapes as flowers, the grey, white and black would have to be seen as symbols of the 'machine age'.

- The propeller motif is reminiscent of the way industrial progress was celebrated in Russian Constructivist design. But what seems to be celebrated here, in an assertive and upbeat (though rather geometrical) way, and against a picture postcard blue (sky?) and yellow (sun?), is a connection between femininity (pink flower) and the machine (monochrome propeller motif), and between hedonistic summer colours and strict, almost mechanical regularity. A picture of the times we live in?

Figure 5.7 shows a pattern design by Clare Perkins. The designer has commented that the design was inspired by a Hungarian poem, 'The Dandelion's Tale', about a dandelion who was granted a wish by a fairy for her son and daughter to return to their homeland by being given wings. Let us try to analyse the colours in this pattern, starting again with the overall parameters and then moving to the contrasts:

- Overall, there is little differentiation. The colours are pale, desaturated, neither particularly dark, nor particularly light and not particularly pure either – the violet seems mixed with blue, the blue with grey. Everything is hazy, diffuse.

- But the colours are highly modulated. There are vertical bands that differ in value; there is an overall kind of graininess; there are lighter downwards streaks; and there are barely discernable, ghostly patterns in the background. This gives a sense of mystery and eeriness.

- The colours are also transparent, giving the whole an ethereal, unworldly feeling.

- Outlined against this background are (1) the words of the poem and the shapes of birds, both whiter and lighter, and harmonizing with the environment; and (2) the dark brown

- shapes of the dandelions carrying the two children, which, though small and insignificant, lost in the haze of greyish blue, are nevertheless sharply delineated against it.

All this, together with the unnerving violet of the sky, quite effectively creates the eerie half-light of a hazardous fairy-tale journey.

In such analyses of colour schemes, we focus first on the individual parameters discussed in the previous section of this chapter, and then try to synthesize them into an interpretation that takes the context into account. Although this is a methodical approach, there clearly is no simple formula for measuring what each parameter contributes to our integrated perception of the whole, let alone for moving from an analysis of the way colour is used to an interpretation. Nevertheless, interpretation will emerge from, and be motivated by, a detailed and exhaustive analysis of the way colour is actually used, rather than being based on a selection of just those features that fit a pre-determined idea.

Exercises

1   In the following extract from *Matisse on Art* (1972: 198–9), Henri Matisse describes the murals and windows he created for the Chapel of the Dominican monastery in Venice, in 1951. Which colour parameters and colour schemes does he mention? Does he ascribe meanings to them, and if so, what meanings? To what extent do you think these meanings are brought about by the meaning potential of the parameters he mentions, and to what extent by the context?

The ceramic panels are composed of large squares of glazed white tile bearing drawings in black outline that decorate them while still leaving them very light. The result is an ensemble of black and white in which the white dominates, with a density that forms a balance with the surface of the opposite wall, which is composed of stained-glass windows that run from the floor to the ceiling, and which express, through their neighbouring forms, an idea of foliage that is always of the same origin, coming from a tree characteristic of the region: the cactus with large oval, spine-covered stalks, which bears yellow and red flowers.

These stained-glass windows are composed of three carefully chosen colours of glass, which are: an ultramarine blue, a bottle green, and a lemon yellow, used together in each part of the stained-glass window. These colours are of quite ordinary quality; they exist as an artistic reality only by their harmony of quantities, which magnifies and spiritualizes them.

To the simplicity of these three constructive colours is added a differentiation of the surface of some of the pieces of glass. The yellow is roughened and so becomes only translucent while the blue and the green remain transparent, and thus completely limpid. This lack of transparency in the yellow stops the mind of the spectator and keeps it within the interior of the chapel, thus forming the foreground of a space that begins in the chapel and then passes through the blue and green to lose itself in the surrounding gardens. Thus when someone inside can look through the glass and see a person coming and going in the garden, only a meter away from the window, that person seems to belong to a completely separate world from that of the chapel.

I write of these windows – the spiritual expression of their colours to me is indisputable – simply to establish the difference between the two long sides of the chapel, which, decorated differently, sustain themselves by their mutual opposition. From a space of bright shadowless sunlight that envelops our spirit on the left, we find, passing to the right, the tile walls. They are the visual equivalent of a large open book where the white pages carry the signs explaining the musical part composed by the stained-glass windows.

In sum, the ceramic tiles are the main spiritual part and explain the meaning of the monument.

. . .

I would like to add to this text that I have included the black and white habits of the Sisters as one of the elements of the composition of the chapel; and, for the music, I preferred to the strident tones of the organ – which are enjoyable but explosive – the sweetness of the voices of women, which with their Gregorian chant can become a part of the quivering coloured light of the stained-glass windows.

2 Choose a surface pattern along the lines of Figures 5.6 and 5.7. It could be a wrapping paper, a fabric or a wallpaper, for instance. Analyse it according to the ideas introduced in this chapter, first observing the parameters and their values, and then attempting to interpret their meaning potential.

3 Make a proportional inventory of an eighteenth-century painting and describe the meaning potential which the resulting colour scheme might have for a contemporary design application of your choice (e.g. fashion, interior design).

6 Colour in Art and Architecture

6.1 Introduction

The Middle Ages have been called the Dark Ages, but medieval art in fact abounded with strong, vibrant colour. Paintings shone with glittering gold, intense blues and luminous reds; mosaics shimmered with iridescent, gemstone-like colours. Stained-glass windows filtered coloured light into the churches; the 'illustrations' and 'illuminations' in manuscripts were exactly what their name suggests – lustrous and luminous.

Renaissance artists and art theorists rediscovered classic authors who had argued for a restrained colour palette, and began to see medieval debates about colour symbolism as meaningless hair-splitting. They wanted to learn how to use colour naturalistically, for creating an illusion of three-dimensionality on a flat surface, for representing depth and for modelling surfaces. The materiality and texture of paint or other materials no longer mattered to them, but what mattered all the more was the art of *representing* materiality in fine and realistic detail, by means of variations in hue and saturation and subtle colour tingeing of shades and shadows. Artists began to study nature, observing how light models and colours objects differently at different times of the day and in different weather conditions. Leonardo's *Notebooks* (Da Vinci, 2005) continue to testify to the sudden surge of new discoveries in this period, many of them as valid today as they were then. At the same time, colour theory became scientific rather than semiotic, concerned with the physics and chemistry rather than the meanings of colour. All this continued until well into the nineteenth century, during what, in Chapter 2, I called the 'monochrome age'.

Although there were some notable colourists before Impressionism (Turner's sometimes luminous, sometimes dark and brooding landscapes, for instance, or the colourful Oriental costumes and ornaments Ingres liked to include in his genre paintings) it was Impressionism that ended the 'monochrome age' and brought colour back. And while the Impressionists still used colours naturalistically, as the true colours of people, places and things they depicted, soon artists would start using colours non-representationally, as a means of expression in its own right, separate from, or in addition to, the objects they were the colours of. In this chapter I will discuss this development, starting with the Impressionists and moving to the abstract art of the first decades of the twentieth century. I will then discuss a further fundamental step that artists took in this period, the move from art to design, in which the forms and colours of abstract art came to be used as the forms and colours of everyday objects such as lamps and chairs, and of the built environment we live in. As Theo van Doesburg, a Dutch artist who played a key role in the De Stijl art movement in the 1920s, put it: '[modern art] places man within the painting instead of in front of it, and thereby enables him to participate in it' (quoted in Overy, 2001: 185).

For many of the artists of this period, art was a form of research. They read the theories of contemporary scientists, psychologists and philosophers, tried them out in their work, and often came up with new ideas as a result, expressed in their art, rather than in words (although many of the most important artists of the period also wrote about their ideas). Van Doesburg explicitly likened the work of these artists to that of research scientists and strongly felt that artists should not only produce, but also explain, their revolutionary innovations. But he also stressed that ideas can be, and are, produced in and through artistic practice rather than that they already exist and are then 'applied' by the artist (quoted in Jaffé, 1967: 10):

> The truly modern – i.e. conscious – artist has a double vocation; in the first place to produce the purely plastic work of art, in the second place to prepare the public's mind for this purely plastic art . . . By the mere fact that the modern artist is able to write about his own work, the prejudice that the modern artist works according to preconceived theories will disappear. On the contrary, it will appear that the new work of art does not derive from theories accepted *a priori*, but rather the reverse, that the principles arise out of creative activity.

Many of the ideas and innovations artists and designers produced in this period are, today, as relevant as they were then. I will discuss them in this chapter, with special emphasis on the colour schemes they created for their art and design work.

6.2 The return of colour in modern art

The Impressionists brought back colour in Western art, using colour rather than drawing as the starting point of visual composition. They were still interested in truthful representation, but they used a new criterion for the truth of painting. The truth they were interested in was not the objective truth of science, but the subjective truth of perception. In this they were influenced by the physicist von Helmholtz, who, in 1855, had said that 'we never perceive the objects of the external world directly'. 'On the contrary', he had said, 'we only perceive the effects of these objects on our own nervous apparatuses, and it has always been like that, from the first moment of our lives (quoted in Gage, 1993: 206). This 'effect on the nervous apparatus' is what the Impressionists wanted to capture. They wanted to 'record sensation', as Cézanne would later put it (*ibid.*: 210). This led to the now well-known but then innovative technique of painting *taches*, small coloured shapes which, on their own, represented nothing, but slowly built up a recognizable representation, just as the coloured pieces of a large jigsaw puzzle at first do not seem to represent anything, but slowly begin to reveal a house, a tree, or the sky, as they are assembled. Monet described the process as follows (*ibid.*: 209):

> When you go out to paint, try to forget what objects you have before you, a tree, a house, a field, or whatever. Merely think, here is a little square of blue, here an oblong of pink, here a streak of yellow, and paint it just as it looks to you, the exact colour and shape, until it gives your own naïve impression of what you see before you.

The Impressionists were also influenced by Chevreul, who, as we saw in Chapter 3, formulated the law of simultaneous contrast (complementary colours strengthen each other; non-complementary colours contaminate each other) and showed that this effect does not only happen in mixing, but also when two flat colours are put side by side, in which case the intensification or contamination is, again, a perceptual effect rather than an objective reality. From this followed the idea of 'optical mixing': instead of actually mixing, for instance green from yellow and blue, it is also possible to put small dots or brush strokes of yellow and blue next to each other, unmixed. From the right distance these will then appear to fuse into a single colour, green – the same principle that also operates in colour printing, as we saw in Chapter 3. In the pointillism of Seurat, this method was most systematically applied – Seurat himself described it in near scientific terms (quoted in Gage, 1999: 209):

> The means of expression is the optical mixture of tonal values and colours (both local colour and the colour of the light source, be it sun, oil lamps, gas, etc.) that is to say, the optical mixture of lights and their reactions (shadows) in accordance with the laws of contrast, gradation and irradiation.

But, as Gage has shown (*ibid.*), this did not mean that he applied his pointillist method mechanically. When he noticed that contrasting values are harder to mix, so that viewers would have to increase their distance from the painting to get the 'optical mixing' effect, he began experimenting with the size of his dots. And when necessary, he helped optical mixing along by darkening the edges of objects set against a light background, and lightening the edges of objects set against a dark background. Rigorous method was balanced by artistic judgement.

The Impressionists also brought back the materiality of paint and painting, but in a new way. They were interested in visible brush strokes and visible dots. Seurat deliberately enlarged his dots in parts of his paintings – he *wanted* them to be seen. In the age of the dematerialized images of photography, the *texture* of paint and painting (rather than the textures of represented objects, as in seventeenth-century Dutch still-life paintings) began to matter again.

Vincent van Gogh took these experiments a step further. Often represented as a tortured, lone genius, Van Gogh, like other artists of his time, was well read, connected to the major artistic and intellectual debates of the period, and interested in the science of colour (quoted in Gage, 1999: 205):

> The laws of colour are unutterably beautiful, just because they are not accidental. In the same way that people nowadays no longer believe in fantastic miracles, no longer believe in a God . . . but begin to feel more respect and admiration for, and faith in, nature, in the same way, and for the same reasons, I think that in art, the old-fashioned idea of genius, inspiration, etc., I do not say must be put aside, but thoroughly reconsidered, verified – and greatly modified.

In his own use of colour, Van Gogh still stood with one foot in the Impressionist period. Like the Impressionists, he wanted to 'reproduce' what he saw. In his letters he describes the colours he sees around him, and his 'sadness' at not being able to 'reproduce' them faithfully (Van Gogh, 1978: 222):

> Nature here is superb, autumn effects glorious in colour, green skies contrasting with foliage in yellows, oranges, greens, earth in all the violets, heat-withered grass among which, however, the rains have given a last energy to certain plants which again start putting forth little flowers of violet, pink, blue, yellow. Things that one is quite sad not to be able to reproduce.

But although he wanted to represent natural colours 'as faithfully as I can', he also started using colour to *express* rather than represent – to express feelings and to symbolize ideas such as, in the following quote, 'infinity', 'mystery', and the terror of a 'terrible furnace' (1978: 6):

> I should like to paint the portrait of an artist friend . . . I paint him as he is, as faithfully as I can, to begin with. But the picture is not yet finished. To finish it, I am now going to be the arbitrary colourist. . . . Behind the head, instead of painting the ordinary wall of the mean room, I paint infinity, a plain background of the richest, intensest blue that I can contrive, and by this simple combination of the bright head against the rich blue background, I get a mysterious effect, like a star in the depth of an azure sky. Again, in the portrait of the peasant I worked this way . . . I imagine the man I have to paint, terrible in the furnace of the height of harvest time . . . hence the orange colours clashing like lightning, vivid as a red-hot iron, and hence the luminous tone of old gold in the shadows.

After Aurier, a contemporary art critic, had praised him as 'the only painter to perceive the chromatism of things with such intensity, with such a metallic, gemlike lustre', he contemplated going even further (*ibid.*: 254): 'Aurier's article would encourage me, if I dared to let myself go, to venture even further, dropping reality and making a kind of music of tones with colour.' But in the end he felt he would rather be a 'shoemaker' than a 'musician in colours' (*ibid.*).

What are the essential characteristics of Van Gogh's colour scheme? First of all, the increasingly strong saturation and purity of his colours. This, more than anything else, expresses the intensity of his vision which, after more than a century, still speaks to us. Second, the modulation created by the visible brush strokes which intermingle lighter and darker values of the same colour, or adjacent colours such as yellow and green. Third, the luminosity of his colours, above all the yellows and oranges which are so characteristic of his work, often offset against blue. And finally, a particular form of differentiation – the clash of complementary colours with which Van Gogh, time and again, sought to express his ideas, expressing, for instance, 'the love of two lovers by a wedding of two complementary colours, their mingling and their opposition, the mysterious vibrations of kindred tones' (*ibid.*: 26). Here is his description of *The Night Café*, reproduced in Figure 6.1:

> I have tried to express the terrible passions of humanity by means of red and green. The room is blood red and dark yellow with a green billiard table in the middle; there are four citron-yellow lamps with a glow of orange and green. Everywhere there is clash and contrast of the most disparate reds and greens . . . the blood red and the yellow-green of the billiard table, for instance, contrast with the soft tender Louis XV green of the counter, in which there is a pink nosegay. The white coat of the landlord, awake in a corner of that furnace, turns citron-yellow, or pale luminous green.

And finally, Van Gogh, too, insisted on showing the materiality of paint and painting. Increasingly his way of applying paint to the canvas became a vigorous, driven handwriting of brisk or curved, flame-like brush strokes, especially in later work such as *The Sower* (1888), *Starry Night* (1889) and *Wheatfield with Crows* (1890) (*ibid.*: 478):

> My brush stroke has no system at all. I hit the canvas with irregular touches of the brush which I leave as they are. Patches of thickly laid-on colour, spots of canvas left uncovered, here and there portions that are left absolutely unfinished, repetitions, savageries.

6.3 Colour and abstraction

Early twentieth-century abstract art went where Van Gogh did not yet dare to go, 'dropping reality altogether'. Around 1917, the artists associated with De Stijl still represented reality, albeit in a geometrically stylized way. Mondrian painted mainly landscapes and buildings and complained that it was difficult to paint a tree using only rectangles (anyone who has tried making a tree with Lego blocks can sympathize). Others, such as Van der Leck and Van Doesburg painted figures and still-lives. But by the 1920s they had all moved to fully abstract compositions. In Germany, at the Bauhaus, where art was to serve as a foundation for creative design, Kandinsky taught his students abstraction – 'precise observation, not of the outward appearance of an object, but of the constructive elements, the tensions of forces' (Fiedler, 2006: 387).

With abstract forms come abstract meanings. Mondrian's compositions sought to balance horizontal lines representing the earth with vertical lines representing the impact of humanity's activities on it (Overy, 2001: 70). Theo van Doesburg saw diagonal lines as uplifting and 'spiritual', because they opposed the gravitational stability of box-like constructions. In Germany, Kandinsky assembled circles, half moons, triangles, and various kinds of rectangles into shapes that were sometimes abstract, sometimes half recognizable as mysterious buildings or mythical animals. The abstract representations of science also inspired artists. Vilmos Huszár, Van Doesburg, Klee and Kandinsky all used chequerboard-like grids, which had been introduced as a tool in psychology by the Berlin psychologist F. Schumann in 1900 (Gage, 1993: 158), to design ordered schemas of colours and relations between colours.

As they sought to reduce the forms of reality to a small vocabulary of abstract shapes, so these artists also sought to reduce colour to a small set of basic colours, often drawing on the scientific colour theories I discussed in Chapter 3. The chemist Ostwald, who was also an amateur painter, was particularly influential, liaising with artists, lecturing in art and design schools and arguing for 'correct' and systematic uses of colour. Artists experimented with these ideas and adapted them for their own purposes, seeking to base a universal language of colour on universal laws of science. Gerrit Rietveld mistakenly believed that the human eye has three receptors, one for red, one for blue and one for yellow. His use of these three colours (plus white, black and grey) was therefore, he thought, based on the natural laws of perception. Vantongerloo based his use of colour on the physics of light, working with Newton's seven spectral colours. Ideas and practices of this kind were hotly debated. Mondrian, for instance, criticized Vantongerloo's seven spectral colours as 'premature': 'With his Belgian intellect he has created an operative system which, as I see it, is based on nature. He hasn't the faintest idea of the difference between the manner of nature and the manner of art' (quoted in Gage, 1993: 259). Mondrian's own reduced palette of pure red, blue and yellow, combined with black and white, evolved only gradually. Around 1918 he still used yellow-green and still mixed his colours with white, following Ostwald, who had said that colours of the same value harmonize well. For this he was criticized by Van Doesburg, who, himself, continued to use orange, violet and green until the early 1930s. In the Bauhaus, Kandinsky, as head of the new school's Wall Painting workshop, introduced both colour science and colour psychology to his students. 'The first part of my task', he told them, 'is to create a kind of ideal colour box for you, in which the colours are set in a well-founded order' (quoted in Fiedler, 2006: 397) and he even conducted an experiment asking Weimar residents to match basic shapes to basic colours. The majority chose a yellow triangle, a red square and a blue circle.

Abstract colours were given abstract meanings. Two sources of meaning were particularly important, colour psychology and theosophy. Many of the ideas of early twentieth-century psychology were picked up, for instance the idea of colour preference (Huszár, in an article in *De Stijl* magazine, said that 'nothing is more subjective than the reaction to colour, which depends on the nature of the individual', (Gage, 1993: 259)); the idea of the emotive meanings of colour which we discussed in Chapter 5 in relation to Kandinsky (e.g. the 'disturbing influence' and 'shrillness' of yellow and the 'complacent' character of green (see Kandinsky, 1977: 37)); and the idea of synaesthesia, the relations between colour, music, smell and taste, a popular topic of psychological research at the time. Kandinsky, for instance, liked to describe colours in musical terms (1977: 38): 'In music a light blue is like a flute; a darker blue a cello; a still darker blue a thundering double bass; and the darkest of all, an organ.' But for artists like Mondrian and Kandinsky colour was not just psychological, it was also, and above all, 'spiritual'. Kandinsky described the 'psychic effect' of colour as 'spiritual vibration' (1977: 23) and for Mondrian colour should 'be freed from individuality and individual sensations' and 'give expression only to the serene emotion of the universal' (quoted in Jaffé, 1967: 54). Coupled with highly rationalized and systematic colour schemes were near-mystical meanings, as in this quote from Mondrian (quoted in Gage, 1993: 257):

> Natural colour is inwardness (light) in its most outward manifestation. Reducing natural colour to primary colour changes the most outward manifestation of colour back to the most inward.

These meanings came from theosophical literature that was popular at the time, such as Rudolf Steiner's *Astral Bodies* and Charles Leadbetter's *Thought Forms*. Mondrian was particularly influenced by a Dutch ex-priest called M.H.J. Schoenmaeker, who sought to reconcile the scientific and the spiritual – exactly what painters like Mondrian were also trying to do.

What were the colour schemes of these artists like? The De Stijl colour scheme of red, yellow and blue eliminated contrasts of value, saturation and modulation, working with plain, pure, saturated, middle value colours. So important was the quest for purity that Mondrian sought the help of Ostwald to get a purer red. Paradoxically this could only be achieved by glazing a bluish transparent crimson over an opaque orange-red (Gage, 1993: 258). Such qualities made the De Stijl colour scheme at once strong and energizing, eradicating the 'faded, fancy, semidark and humiliating shades' that had dominated the nineteenth century, *and* de-individualized, dematerialized, ready for the mass production of designer objects that would follow. Differentiation, finally, is at once maximal, since the extreme points of the colour compass are all included, and reduced, rationalized, as all intermediate shades and nuances are eliminated.

Kandinsky and Klee, on the other hand, continued to experiment with modulation and transparency, never quite reconciling the scientific rationality they introduced in their teaching with the romantic, individualistic side of their artistic inspiration. Klee had critiqued Ostwald for not taking the subjective effects of colour into account, warning that 'laws should only be a ground in which something can bloom' (quoted in Fiedler, 2006: 351). His watercolours include subtly modulated earth colours, soft greens and abstract shapes coloured in with rainbows of 'impure', pale pinks, mauves, blues and yellows each presenting their own colour scheme, exploring all the values of all the parameters of colour. His *Static Dynamic Gradation* (1929) shows a chequerboard of different colours moving from dark, muddy blacks, browns and greens on the outer edges, towards lighter and purer colours in the centre (see Figure 6.2). All colours are repeated several times, sometimes individually, sometimes in groups, and distributed symmetrically across the grid. In all there are 24 colours, including white, a relatively pure blue and red, and a relatively strong orange, but the yellows are dulled and there are no violets or strong greens. It is a unique 'once only' colour scheme, asking for a specific explanation – the colours of a flag (orange, red, white, blue) embedded in a dull and dark urban landscape, but by being taken out of context creating a more general statement about Germany in the 1920s?

A later movement, Abstract Expressionism, returned to the questions these artists had engaged with in the early twentieth century. As the name implies, Abstract Expressionism relates on the one hand to abstraction, to reducing colour to the basics and the universals and, on the other hand, to expression, to using the full meaning potential of colour for the expression of subtle and complex feelings and symbolic meanings. Mark Rothko was one of these Abstract-Expressionist painters, and, unlike Mondrian, he stressed the affective, expressive side of the equation. He wanted his work to be understood as 'tragedies' and spoke of his paintings as 'mood pictures' (Moszynska, 1990: 167). In a painting like *Red on Maroon*, this translates into colours that are dark, a little desaturated, warm, mixed, modulated, restrained in range (low differentiation) and luminous, therefore setting up a meaning potential that combines the dark and brooding, the complex and subtle (modulation), and the restrained (low differentiation) and ambivalent (red mixed with blue), with the deeply felt (warm colours) and illuminating, almost otherworldly (luminosity). In addition, Rothko's paintings are large, and, in accordance with his very specific wishes, usually shown in rooms that exhibit his work only and are somewhat dimly lit. The effect is hard to describe, but it certainly affects the viewer emotively.

Barnett Newman's work verges less towards the abstract than Mondrian's and less towards the expressive than Rothko's. In *Onement 1* (Figure 6.3), his breakthrough painting, and the first to display the characteristic 'zip', the colour is a dark Indian red split by the orange zip. The orange stripe has a thick impasto and the dark and modulated colour of the two fields has a kind of grain that gives it a sense of materiality.

Cathedra (1951), a five-metre-long work has a still somewhat dark, but much less 'impure' blue, a modulated textured surface with a kind of black staining, and a high degree of luminosity and transparency. It therefore displays a Rothko-like expressiveness, though already with a purer (and a much more ethereal) colour. And, as in Rothko's paintings, the edges are ragged and irregular, rather than striving towards Mondrian-like precision.

In later work, Newman began to reject this approach as too 'picturesque' and started asking himself a more difficult question: If, just like Mondrian, I restrict myself to the basic primaries, and to all three of them, without any modulation or variation in value, can I still be expressive? The outcome of this quest was a series of paintings with the title *Who is Afraid of Red, Yellow and Blue?* (Figure 6.4). All 'picturesque-ness' is eliminated here: no more grain-like texture or mottling, no bias for the coldness of blue or the warmth of red or some other part of the spectrum, no more subtle mixing. Yet in these paintings he worked and layered the colours more than ever before. Standing before the very large paintings, you sense their vibrancy and luminosity, even though, reproduced, the colours might seem flat and lacking in luminosity. These are colours in all their material power, all their proud brilliance as colours. In later paintings he continued this style but began to give the paintings different kinds of titles to lend the colours, and the feelings expressed, a mythical, ancient or sacred character – *Queen of the Night*, *White Fire*, *Anna's Light*, *Jericho*.

This is what Newman himself said about the 'Who is Afraid' series (Newman, 1990: 192):

I was confronting the dogma that colour must be reduced to the primaries, red, yellow and blue. Just as I had confronted other dogmatic positions of the purists, neoplasticists, and other formalists, I was now in confrontation with their dogma, which had reduced red, yellow and blue into an idea-didact, or at best had made them picturesque. Why give in to these purists and formalists who have put a mortgage on red, yellow and blue, transforming these colours into an idea that destroys them as colours? I had therefore the double incentive of using these colours to express what I wanted to do – of makings these colours expressive rather than didactic and freeing them from the mortgage. Why should anybody be afraid of red, yellow and blue?

As is clear from the quote above, Newman, like all the other artists discussed in this chapter, also expressed his ideas in words, and very eloquently at that. He had in fact been an art critic before he became a painter and continued to write throughout his life. But while Newman clearly saw his work as 'philosophic' and as 'an art of ideas', others did not follow suit. The philosopher Lyotard (quoted in Benjamin, 1989: 8) has said that Newman's paintings 'speak of nothing' and 'emanate from no-one':

The message is the presentation but it presents nothing . . . Everything is there – dimensions, colours, lines – but there are no allusions. So much so that it is a problem for the commentator. What can one say that is not given? It is not difficult to describe, but the description is a flat paraphrase.

Lewison, another commentator (2002: 15) takes a different line. Taking one sentence from Newman out of context (the sentence 'I realized that I'd made a statement'), he writes:

In not immediately realizing what he had done, Newman was no different from any other artist who sets out to communicate something without being able to define exactly what it is. At their most adventurous, artists will be on the edge between control and uncontrol, trying to extract something new and unexpected.

And he goes on to say that while Newman's work '*seems* so classical, structured and premeditated' (my emphasis), it is in fact just as intuitive as that of any other artist. Having established this, he sets up a very different motive for Newman's work, not a dialogue with ideas about colour, but a 'quest for wholeness, a search for salvation in the postwar period of uncertainty and anxiety' (*ibid.*: 18). In refusing to engage with Newman's work as a discourse about, and an investigation into, colour, such commentators miss an important aspect of his work. The one, Lyotard, not only seems to lack the ability to read these paintings, but also does not take the trouble to read what the painter himself has to say about them. The other, Lewison, denies Newman the status of a thinker and an experimenter which, like many other key artists of the twentieth century, he so explicitly claimed for himself and reverts to the stereotyped opposition of intuitive inspiration and methodical work which Van Gogh already rallied against, as if not all important and innovative work, whether in semiotic theory or in artistic practice, of necessity must always combine these two.

6.4 Colour in design and architecture

Once abstract artists had reduced the manifold forms and colours of reality to a restricted vocabulary of basic shapes and colours, these shapes and colours could be used as building blocks for product design, architecture and other forms of design which, until then, had been regarded as crafts. Representation changed into making, art into design. Both the Bauhaus and the De Stijl group played a crucial role in this transition. The Bauhaus school of art and design, founded in 1919 by the architect Walter Gropius, trained students in the theory and practice of modern art, not for its own sake, but to instil in them the experimental and imaginative spirit necessary to create innovative design solutions – to 'build' ('Bauhaus' literally means 'building house'). In the first Bauhaus manifesto, Gropius wrote (Fiedler, 2006: 192):

> Architects, sculptors, painters, we must all return to craft. . . . The Bauhaus strives to bring together all artistic creativity in a unity, to unite all craft-based artistic disciplines – sculpture, painting, applied art and craft – as inseparable components of a new art of building.

Materiality was important as a source of inspiration for creative design. In their first-year course with colour theorist Johannes Itten, students had to close their eyes and feel the texture of a range of materials. As Itten explained (Fiedler, 2006: 365):

> As an introduction, long lists of different materials such as wood, glass, textiles, bark, pelts, metal and stone were recorded. Then I had the optical and tactile qualities of these materials assessed. It was not enough simply to recognize the qualities, the characteristics of the materials had to be experienced and described. Contrasts such as smooth-rough, hard-soft and light-heavy not only had to be seen but also felt.

Another Bauhaus teacher, Moholy-Nagy, also stressed materiality (*ibid.*: 376): 'keyboard scales from hard to soft, smooth to rough, warm to cold, firm-edged to amorphous, smooth-polished to sticky-absorbent' and 'optical material scales running from tight to loose-knit; transparent to translucent to opaque; clear to cloudy to dense'. Bauhaus workshops focused on the materialities of product design – joinery, weaving, metal work, ceramics, as well as on wall painting, printing and advertising, photography and architecture. Although the Bauhaus existed for only 14 years (it was closed down by the Nazis in 1933), it is still the single most influential moment in the history of modern design, and some of the designs produced by Bauhaus designers are still in production, and still look modern and stylish, for instance the tubular chairs of Martin Breuer and the 'Barcelona' armchair of Mies van der Rohe.

As for the artists of De Stijl, they also believed that art should merge into the design of everyday objects, and into architecture. As Van Doesburg wrote in 1924 (quoted in Koolhaas *et al.*, 2001: 253):

> We have established the true place of colour in architecture and so declare that painting without architectural construction (that is easel painting) has no further reason for existence.

The De Stijl artists all did commissioned work. Van Doesburg and Huszár worked with architects on colour schemes and took on interior decoration jobs for private clients. Van der

Leck designed rugs, wall hangings, ceramics and tiles, and even packaging and carrier bags (Overy, 2001: 93). Even Mondrian worked as an interior decorator for some time in 1926. Gerrit Rietveld, a furniture maker who had also studied design and architecture, began to produce children's toys from rectangular pieces of timber painted in red, yellow and blue, as well as the now famous 'Rietveld chair', which along with his 'Zigzag chair', is still being produced by the Italian firm Cassina. His Schröder House exemplified 'the simultaneous creation of colour and architecture' (*ibid.*: 116) which Van Doesburg had insisted on, and used grey, white and black together with red, yellow and blue on its exterior as well as in its interior. Outside, windows and the girders supporting the balconies were painted in the primaries. Inside most walls were grey or off-white, but some were (a relatively pale) yellow. The blinds were blue and the floor coverings had a pattern of grey, black, red and white rectangles.

A 1923 De Stijl exhibition in Paris was seen by the famous architect Le Corbusier. In a short article published in the modern art magazine *L'Esprit Nouveau*, he discussed the exhibition with Fernand Léger, who was enthused: 'A red wall, a blue wall, a yellow wall, a black floor or a blue or red or yellow one, I see a total transformation of interior decoration', he said (quoted in De Heer, 2008: 213). But Le Corbusier was less enthusiastic. Although in his younger years, when he was a painter, he had used exuberant colour, inspired by Balkan folk pottery (colour, he wrote at the time, 'exists for the caress and intoxication of the eye' (1987b: 16)), in his architecture he had adopted a 'purist' style, dominated by white and glass. Colour, he felt, would destroy form (*ibid.*):

When a house is completely white, its forms are clear and undiminished, its volumes sharply delineated; its colour clear and simple. The white of chalk is absolute. It makes everything clear . . . It is unambiguous and honest.

Le Corbusier did not entirely abandon colour, but he used it pragmatically, to influence the perception of space, for instance – it had long been realized that blue 'recedes' and creates a sense of spaciousness, while red 'stays in place'. In Pessac, in 1925–26, he built a housing estate of relatively small houses, which had to be closely huddled together to fit on the available land. To create a sense of space he painted one row of houses blue, so that they would 'move towards the horizon', and the houses that flanked them a reddish brown, as this would anchor them firmly in the foreground. Colour can also mask complex arrangements or mistakes, according to Le Corbusier. Overly complex details can be given a drab and inconspicuous colour, and a strong colour can be used nearby, to distract the eye. Finally, colour has psychological effects – blue relaxes, red energizes. In this Le Corbusier followed the colour psychology of the period which I discussed in Chapter 2. But in all other ways, he felt, colour had to be used sparingly. Le Corbusier's purism, with its vast expanses of white and glass, eventually came to be known as 'the International Style' and would dominate architecture until well into the 1960s.

Although Le Corbusier, in the mid-1920s, had spoken out strongly against the use of wallpaper ('Every citizen must replace his hangings, his damasks, his wallpapers, his stencils, with a plain coat of white ripolin' (Le Corbusier, 1987a: 188)), in the early 1930s he accepted a commission from wallpaper manufacturer Salubra to design a colour scheme for wallpapers. By then he had realized that strong, washable wallpapers had advantages over painting, as they could cover the inevitable cracks and other defects in interior walls. He selected 43 plain colours and presented them in what he called 'keyboards' (see Figure 6.5). There were 12 such keyboards, with names such as 'Universe', 'Sand', 'Landscape' and

'Velvet'. Each had a 'base colour' in three different values (see the green bands in Figure 6.5) and 14 other tones.

Most of the colours of the 'Landscape' keyboard are relatively light. In the 1920s, progressive people favoured light, airy interiors, and did away with the 'faded, semidark and humiliating shades' of the nineteenth century. They are also relatively desaturated and impure – earth colours in several values dominate. Differentiation is reduced to natural greens and earth, with just a touch of red. And finally, they are unmodulated and matt – texture and lustre will derive from the play of light and shadow in the environment in which the wallpapers will be used, rather than from the colours themselves. The other keyboards follow the same pattern. The 'Sky' keyboard, for instance, combines pale blues with earth colours and warm greys in different values, adding just one red. But three of the keyboards are different, more extravagant (*bigarrées*) with a wide variation of strong, saturated colours. 'No need to look for any intention here', Le Corbusier explained, 'One has to be content with arbitrary encounters and curious, sharp, even offensive connections' (quoted in De Heer, 2008: 237).

Le Corbusier's colour schemes were innovative. They brought representation back into colour, in a new way, reconnecting design colours with the colours of nature. The 'Landscape' and 'Sky' colours are just that – the many possible shades of the earth and its vegetation, and of the sky in different weathers, with just the one red accent added. And the 'keyboards' as a whole were structured along an opposition between these natural colours ('the major scale', as Le Corbusier said) and what he called the 'disturbing' colours that can provide an accent, or a bit of spice, or a touch of dissonance. In this they foreshadowed contemporary corporate colour schemes and the colour schemes of semiotic software such as PowerPoint, as we will see in Chapter 7.

In architecture, such colour schemes would not return until the Postmodern 1970s and 80s. Architect Michael Graves, for instance, used blue to allude to the sky, green to allude to foliage, and brown to allude to earth in an addition to the Schulman house which he built in 1976 (quoted in Riley, 1995: 213):

> The addition has been polychromed to reflect its relation to the garden or landscape. An attempt was made to root the building in the ground by placing the representation of the garden, dark green, at the base of the façade. Next, a terra cotta belt coursing has been used to register the idea of the raised ground plane or ground floor within the house. The green façade is continued above to suggest the addition as a garden room but is given a lighter value as if washed by light. The composition is capped by a blue cornice with a second minor belting of terra cotta, suggesting the juxtaposition to the soffit or sky.

Other Postmodern architects used colour to make strong, provocative statements, as in the red and blue tubes of Renzo Piano's Pompidou Centre in Paris, or in James Stirling's 1984 modern art addition to the Stuttgart Staatsgalerie, which featured what *New York Times* architecture critic Paul Goldberger called an 'electric green', and others a 'bilious green', a 'poison green', a 'jungle-like glow' and a 'translucent green that virtually screams' (Riley, 1995: 217):

> The museum is . . . a dazzling mixture of rich stone and bright – even garish – colour. Its façade is a series of terraces of stone, stripes of sandstone and brown travertine marble, mounting upward as they set back, and it is punctuated by huge tubular metal railings of blue and magenta and by undulating window walls framed in electric green.

Yet other architects began to focus on reflected colour. Norman Foster's Willis Faber & Dumas building in Ipswich had green carpets throughout. As Overy describes it (2001: 126):

> By day, the three serpentine stories of suspended solar tinted glass reflect the colours of the buildings across the street and the sky. At night this reflective skin melts away to reveal the lit-up interior and the greenish glow of artificial light, bounced off the surfaces of green floor coverings and green-painted service plants.

Here colour results from the environment and changes as the environment changes, making it luminescent as well as evanescent, ever-changing.

In the 1990s, architecture became monochrome again, with at best a single strong colour sparingly applied in otherwise neutrally tinted environments. Yet the new interest in the colour of fleeting reflections and colourful illuminations continued, lighting up our cities with ever-changing reflections and ethereal light displays on glass-topped skyscrapers (see Figure 6.6). As architect Rem Koolhaas has commented (Koolhaas *et al.*, 2001: 11):

> With minimalism in the nineties it was at most the inherent colour of materials themselves that was allowed to register – a kind of colourless colour of subtle hints and refined contrasts. As if anything more was too much for our refined nervous systems. But maybe colour could make a comeback – not the exuberant intensity of the sixties and seventies, but with more impact than the sedated nineties – simply through the impact of new technologies and new effects. In a world where nothing is stable, the permanence of colour is slightly naïve.

Exercises

1   What, according to the following extract from Michel Pastoureau (2008: 184), is novel and 'post-minimalist' about the work of Pierre Soulages? Can you explain Soulages' approach to black in terms of the colour parameters introduced in Chapter 5? Can you think of examples of contemporary fashion or product design that use a similar approach to black?

> The return to black expanded after World War I, when abstraction provided fertile ground for it. . . . By the 1920s to 1930s, black became or returned to being a fully 'modern' colour, as did the (so-called) primary colours: red, yellow, blue. On the other hand, white and especially green were regarded differently and were never granted that status. For certain abstract artists (let us think of Mondrian or Miró, for example), green was no longer a basic colour, a colour in its own right. This was a new idea, contradicting all the social and cultural uses for the colour green for centuries, even millennia.

> With regard to black, it would be a few decades before a painter arrived on the scene who would devote nearly all his work to it: Pierre Soulages (born in 1929). From the 1950s, black, applied with a spatula and the line traced with a knife constituted his principal means of expression. The gesture of the painter took on considerable importance because it determined how the material spread across the canvas became a form. Black was largely dominant, but it was often combined with one or many other more discreet colours. Beginning in the years 1975–1980, Pierre Soulages moved from black to *outrenoir*, a term he himself invented to characterize

a 'beyond of black'. Henceforth most of his canvases were entirely covered in a subtle, uniform ivory black, worked with fine and coarse brushes to give it a texture that according to the light produced a great variety of luminous effects and coloured nuances, It was not at all a matter of monochromy, but of an extremely subtle mono-pigmentary practice producing through reflections an infinity of luminous images interposed between the viewer and the canvas. This was a unique case in the whole history of painting, a magnificent extreme case which had nothing to do with the harrowing *Black Squares* of the minimalist artist Ad Reinhardt (1913–67), uniform black rectangles devoid of any texture and lacking any aesthetic ambition.

2   Photograph three buildings and analyse their colour schemes in terms of the parameters introduced in Chapter 5, noting resemblances to and differences from at least three of the colour schemes discussed in this chapter.

3   Paint three identical small objects (e.g. wooden boxes with sliding lids), using a different colour scheme for each, and basing yourself in each case on one of the colour schemes discussed in this chapter. What different uses do the different colour schemes suggest, and what kind of users do you think they might appeal to?

7 Colour in Contemporary Life

7.1 Colour and identity

Two types of colour meaning have come to play a particularly important role in contemporary life: identity meaning and textual meaning. I will discuss each in turn in this final chapter.[1]

Colour has, of course, always played an important role in signifying identity (cf. the discussion of medieval heraldry in Chapter 2, for instance). The Prague School semiotician Bogatyrev (1971[1937]) described the use of colour in the traditional dress of Moravian Slovakia. Colour could tell you much about the wearer's identity – where he or she came from, for instance. There were 28 costume districts in Moravian Slovakia, and you could instantly recognize a man from Pozlovice because of the carmine and green ribbons on his hat, while a man from Biskupice, for instance, would wear only one red ribbon. It could also tell you the social class of the wearer. Squires wore bright blue breeches, for instance, peasants black or coarse white ones. And it could tell you the age and marital status of the wearer. In the Mutinece-Novorany district, unmarried men wore hats with red and white ribbons and narrow rims, while married men would widen the rim and wear a broad gold band. In short, colour provided what we now call 'demographic' information, the kind of information you have to fill in on forms: age, gender, place of domicile, marital status, profession, etc.

But alongside this kind of *social identity*, there is also *individual identity* – the unique identity of each individual, and colour can play a role here as well. I might for instance habitually wear monochrome grey outfits, regardless of fashion, and regardless of my station in life and the dress codes of my place of work, say a grey suit, an off-white shirt, a tie without a speck of colour. Together with other features of the way I dress and present myself, such neutral colours can become my 'trademark', making me instantly recognizable, even to people who do not know my name, and expressing aspects of my personality – perhaps I wear grey because I am a modest person, a person who does not want to stand out from the crowd. The personal palettes of artists can also be said to express individual identity in this way, though they are usually created more deliberately.

Contemporary *lifestyle identity*, finally, is identity in terms of what people *do*, especially in their leisure time, what newspapers they read, what movies they go to, what music they listen to, what sports they play or watch, where they go on holiday etc., and in terms of their 'attitudes', the causes they espouse, and, above all, the consumer goods they buy. In other words, it is identity in terms of the kind of profiles marketing experts draw up. Here are two examples, from an article in the lifestyle section of *The Guardian* (12 March 2004):

'Ties of community'

This group lives in very established, rather old-fashioned communities. Traditionally they marry young, work in manual jobs and have strong social support networks with friends and relatives living nearby. There is a sub-type of this group called Coronation Street, but not all Lee and Noreens live in back-to-back terraces or keep pigeons. Likely to shop at Morrisons, Asda, Kwik Save.

'Urban intelligence'

Young, well educated, liberal, childless and well off. They are mindful of career uncer-tainties but are often involved in high risk investments such as the buy-to-let market. Not all of them read *The Guardian*; many are in lifestyle thrall to Sarah Beeny. Likely to shop at Sainsbury's.

On the one hand this form of identity is individual. It is freely chosen rather than socially imposed. People see it as an expression of 'who they are', individually. On the other hand it is social, because lifestyle choices are shared with other people, and expressed through appearances (styles of dress and adornment, interior decoration, and so on) hence by socially produced, 'off the shelf' consumer goods:

> Strongly held beliefs and commitment to family values are likely to be symbolized by particular types of aesthetic choice, just as militant feminism is likely to be associated with particular ways of dressing, talking and leisure.
>
> (Chaney, 1996: 98)

Compared to social and individual style, it is also a relatively unstable form of identity, a form of identity that can change with the winds of fashion, and whose latest signifiers therefore need to be carefully monitored in lifestyle magazines, newspaper supplements, television makeover programmes and social media, if we are to keep up to date with its constantly evolving forms and contents.

The signifiers of lifestyle rest predominantly on connotation, on signs that are already loaded with cultural meaning but not yet subject to prescription or tradition. More specifically, they rest on *composites of connotation*. Connotation is here understood as based on provenance, on 'where things come from'. An object (e.g. a garment) or a quality of an object (e.g. a colour) is then recognized as coming from a particular context (a particular culture, a particular historical period, a particular activity, a particular group, etc.), and conveys ideas and values that are commonly associated with that context in popular culture and hence familiar to anyone who is at all exposed to mass media. Perhaps this is best explained by an example. The model in a *Vogue* fashion spread (*American Vogue*, January 2010, p. 135) wears a mini-dress. We know that the mini-skirt came into fashion in the 1960s, a period of change in women's lives (women's liberation, the pill, a certain relaxation of sexual mores, etc.). The fabric, however, is black and white tweed, a fabric more often associated with conservative, older women. Sewn onto the dress are flak vest type pockets, in military brown. From the model's bag hangs a fox tail, like a kind of hunting trophy. The whole outfit therefore is a composite of connotations. It combines sexual provocation and conservativeness with military and hunting connotations. It says: if you wear this, you are sexy, yet conservative, as well as tough and a bit wild, a fighter and a hunter (Sarah Palin fashion?). The accompanying text sums it up: the model is dressed for a 'tactile manoeuvre' (note the pun, fusing 'tactile' and 'tactical', just as the dress fuses the sexy and the military). Clearly someone wearing this dress does not signify her social position or unique personal style, but a set of ideas and values, and a certain, currently fashionable, type of female identity which, unlike social identity, can be adopted and discarded at will. Its signifiers have been taken out of the environments in which they once signified age, gender and class (the black and white tweed) and a profession (the military) to signify values typically associated with, but not necessarily confined to, these environments ('conservativeness' and 'fighting spirit').

This use of colour now plays a fundamental role in the communication of identity, both of individuals and of corporations and other organizations. To add a corporate example, the logo, the lettering on aircrafts, and the uniforms of THAI airlines use gold, magenta and purple. The logo is a rather solid and massive kind of arrow (indicating 'solidity' as well as 'dynamism' (see THAI, 2010)), but it has the curves of traditional Thai design, indicating 'elegance' (*ibid*.). The colours, like those of the *Vogue* outfit convey identity through 'where they come from' – they 'reflect the culture and the country' and 'recall the gold of temples, the intensity of Thailand's famous shimmering silks and the brilliant hues of the orchids' (*ibid*.). Just as the shape of the logo conveys the key values of the brand ('solidity, elegance and dynamism'), so the colours convey the national identity that is enshrined in the airline's name, and the values associated with that identity.

7.2 Normative discourses

Throughout this book I have stressed that the same colours can have different meanings in different contexts. Colour meaning does not emerge naturally, on the basis of intuitive understandings. Normative discourses are therefore needed to make the forms and contents of colour meaning explicit, especially in the case of lifestyle meanings, which are unstable and subject to fashion. Colours which yesterday were dull and unfashionable might, tomorrow, be back in fashion, and this cannot be brought about without a constant barrage of commentaries on colour and its meanings in lifestyle magazines, newspaper supplements, advertisements, television makeover programmes and internet media. Three types of normative discourse play a particularly important role here: authoritative discourses, expert discourses, and role modelling. I will discuss them in turn.

Authority

Authoritative discourses impose norms for the use of colour without any form of justification. Colour codes, for instance, might simply be prescribed, as in the case of the rules for academic dress of the University of Newcastle ('the academic dress . . . shall be:'):

> The academic dress for graduates of the University shall be:
>
> Doctors of Architecture, Doctors of Education, Doctors of Engineering, Doctors of Law, Doctors of Letters, Doctors of Medicine, Doctors of Music, Doctors of Nursing, Doctors of Science, Doctors of the University – a festal gown of cardinal red cloth, with a hood of garnet cloth lined with silk cloth of the appropriate colour namely:
>
>> Doctors of Architecture – deep indian red
>> Doctors of Business – turquoise
>> Doctors of Education – jade
>> Doctors of Engineering – lapis lazuli
>> Doctors of Law – waratah
>> (etc.)

Corporate colours, too, may be prescribed authoritatively and without explanation (HSBC, 2006):

Wherever possible HSBC corporate signatures should be reproduced in black and HSBC red on white or very light background colours. The interior of the hexagon symbol must be white.

Even lifestyle colour meaning might be prescribed in this way. In his book *The Fashion System* (1983), Roland Barthes analysed the captions of magazine fashion spreads as, among other things, unilaterally declaring that something or other is 'now' ('this season') in fashion (references to the seasons and the weather represent changes in fashion as a quasi-natural phenomenon). More than 40 years after he first noted this, his observations are still valid:

From military jackets to feathery skirts, these are the top five trends you'll be wearing this season.
(*Sydney Magazine*, April 2010: 79)

Dark denim washes make a comeback as the weather cools.
(*Cosmopolitan*, January 2010: 182)

Often the language of the imperative is used – people are *told* what to do:

Stay cool and look hot in minis that show off your legs.
(*Cosmopolitan*, January 2010: 165)

Tough enough! Work leather into your casual wardrobe, but use it sparingly.
(*Cleo Australia*, January 2010: 141)

As well as declaring things to be 'in fashion' and telling people what to wear, such captions also index fashion meanings, including colour meanings, for instance in terms of 'personality traits' ('wild', 'glamorous', 'sexy', etc.) or in terms of the occasions for which the fashions are suitable. These meanings are therefore also unilaterally and authoritatively announced:

Sharp cuts and wild animal prints will help you look the part in the corporate jungle.
(*Sydney Magazine*, March 2010: 79)

For a sexy Miami vibe, turn up the heat in these daring, layered looks.
(*Cosmopolitan*, January 2010: 138)

All this is, of course, written in playful, tongue-in-cheek fashion, avoiding the authoritative tone of the rule-book. As with all irony, this at once gets the message across and disavows fashion's power to decide what people will be wearing 'this season'.

Expertise

Expert advice is another type of normative discourse. The psychological colour expertise which, as I argued in Chapter 2, has its origins in Goethe's colour theory, is still the most dominant form of colour expertise, although it might now be overtaken by a more semiotic kind of colour expertise which consists of a wide knowledge of the ways in which specific colours have been used in the past and in other cultures. Such cultural-historical knowledge can be used in both interpretation and creation. Cultural critics and social semioticians can use it to understand the meanings of colour. Designers can use it as inspiration for new recontextualizations of old colour meanings. This example, from a recent article in which a magazine 'invited five colour experts to answer some of our most-often asked questions', however, shows that traditional 'psychological' colour expertise still has currency, especially in interior decoration (*Vogue Living, Before and After* 2010: 41):

> I think bedrooms are better in cooler colours which are calmer. Kitchens look good in fresh, clean colours on the warm side because the kitchen is the 'heart' of the home. I usually choose richer warmer colours for a study.

In another example, 'Leatrice Eiseman, author of The Color Answer Book', revives 1920s' colour therapy (*Cosmopolitan*, November 2004: 110):

> These four shades provide major mood-boosting benefits
>
> Red increases your heart rate and excites sexual glands, so you'll get giddy . . . and maybe a little horny. If a lack of motivation is dragging you down, orange will come to your aid. It's the Energizer Bunny of brights. Let the sunshine in! Soaking up a sunny shade of yellow can relieve depression and improve your memory . . . so you can reminisce about all the good times you've had. Mint green is seriously soothing. Read: You'll be too relaxed to dwell on life's downers.

The media might also nominate fashion designers, interior decorators and architects as experts, explicitly credentialing them in the articles that display their expertise, with full contact details of their offices. In the example below, the expert is at the same time a role model, as she describes her own house.

> Interior designer Jane Charlwood knows what she likes: calm, understated interiors and a classic, muted palette of taupe, grey and white: 'I'm an all-white girl, really', she says, 'I'm obsessed by light'.
>
> (*Vogue Living Before and After* 2010: 80)

This introduction is then followed by the details of a colour scheme that favours 'simplicity', 'airiness', 'light' and 'peace and quiet' (*ibid.*: 85):

> Adding spice to the classic greys and taupe colours is an orange Cassina 'Utrecht' armchair by Gerrit Rietveld, its tangerine tones picked up throughout the room – in a painting, a vase, a cushion. 'The spaces called out for splashes of colour,' says Charlwood, 'You can add accent colours and take them away when you get sick of them . . . Upstairs, where Charlwood retreats for 'more peace and quiet', there is very little colour. The bathroom is treated with all white surfaces in Thassos marble, with large windows overlooking the garden. Charlwood's only concession to retaining the exposed walls is in the bedroom where the walls are painted in Dulux 'Grand Piano'. Ceiling rafters were painted in white gloss to pick up the light.

In other cases, such experts describe houses they have designed for their clients (*ibid.*: 119):

> All three bedrooms have private decks, and the master showcases [interior designer] Bechara's gentle approach in melding feminine and masculine design elements. A

transparent plissé curtain and wide lamp in blush pink tones contrast softly against the sand-hued bed and an armchair version of the Brazilian leather sofa. 'I sought to give a strong balance of the masculine and feminine, retro and contemporary that's also refined,' says Bechara, 'Blending the bold and the understated is the key to my process'.

Role models

'Role model' discourses communicate norms through 'best practice examples' in which celebrities model the latest fashions, beauty and fitness regimes and so on, for instance in magazine articles which at the same time profile the role models and provide sufficient instructional detail to allow readers to follow their example. The articles first introduce the model (*Cosmopolitan*, January 2010: 176):

> With her character Vanessa Abrams getting meatier scenes on hit show *Gossip Girl*, and having recently wrapped a movie – *Piranha 3-D*, due out next year – hard-working Jessica Szohr, 24, is finally getting the attention she deserves. With her exotic looks, thanks to Hungarian and African-American heritage, Szohr (pronounced Zoar), the eldest of five from small-town Menomonee Falls in Wisconsin, is also becoming known for her off-camera style – not including her best accessory ever, boyfriend and co-star Ed Westwick.

After having introduced Jessica, the article moves to a close description of her wardrobe and make up style, in which meanings ('simple', 'edgy') are casually embedded, more or less in the same way as they are in fashion captions (*ibid.*: 177):

> When I use makeup I'm very simple. I like bronzing and I like blush. I like Laura Mercier bronzer – her foundation is incredible as well. I wear black nail polish a lot. It kind of goes with everything; it's a little bit of an edge.

Authority and expert discourses are still widely used, as my recent examples in the previous sections show. Nevertheless, role modelling (which of course has a well-established pedigree in advertising) is gradually becoming the dominant way of providing lifestyle identity norms. Many magazines have replaced old-style advice columns, in which a single expert provides authoritative solutions, with 'hot tips columns' that allow a choice between solutions and a variety of 'role model articles profiles' can also provide this kind of choice. In the age of personal media such as *Facebook*, personalized profiles of likeable celebrities are perhaps more attractive than 'mass media' approaches which prescribe fashion more authoritatively and bindingly An added advantage is that many celebrities come with ready-made lifestyle meanings, established by the characters they have played in films or television series, the kinds of lyrics they sing, or, simply, the stories that are told about them in the media. For fans of *Gossip Girl*, the meanings of the colours Jessica Szohr uses in the *Cosmopolitan* shoot might need no explanation – the fact that *she* is wearing them might communicate them without words.

Ordinary people can also function as role models, for instance Hamish and Vanessa in *House Beautiful Magazine* (September 1998: 20). Again, they are introduced before their home is described.

> Guessing what Hamish and Vanessa Dows do for a living isn't too difficult – a pair of feet on the house number plate is a dead giveaway for a couple who are both chiropodists, but it's also an indication of the fun they've had in decorating their home.

A little later we learn, among other things, that Hamish and Vanessa:

> used nearly the whole spectrum in their house, from mustard yellow and leaf green in the sitting room, to brick red and blue in the dining room. Their bedroom is a soft buttery yellow combined with orange, there's lemon and lime in the breakfast room and cornflower and Wedgwood blues on the stairs. 'I think it's great there are so many bright shades in the house', says Hamish, 'It's a shame people aren't more adventurous with this use of colour. It's when you start being timid that things go wrong.'

This quote gives a description of the colours, the fact that they range across the spectrum (i.e. high differentiation) and are 'bright' (i.e. high saturation), as well as their meanings – 'adventurous', 'not timid'. There is motivation – it is easy to see why these particular signifiers ('multi-coloured' and 'bright') should have potential for meaning 'adventurous' and why their opposite, a single pale colour, could be said to be more 'timid'. And the colours, again, signify 'personality traits'. Hamish and Vanessa use their home to signify identity, to show what kind of people they are – they are 'adventurous', 'not afraid to choose bright shades', 'always confident about their choices' (*ibid.*: 20).

However, a closer look at the colours themselves reveals that the colour scheme is not quite as bright as they make out. The colours are relatively dark and 'impure' and somewhat desaturated (Figure 7.1). Such colours were very much in fashion in the 1990s, and they had a specific provenance in the historical television series that were popular in the Britain at the time. They are, in fact, an exact match to some of the historic colours on the colour chart of a paint manufacturer called Farrow & Ball, a specialist firm which produced authentic colours for the television adaptations of *Pride and Prejudice* and *Middlemarch* and subsequently saw the sales of these paints to domestic customers rise by 40 per cent each year over a ten-year period (*Guardian Weekend Magazine*, 19 January 2002: 67).

Perhaps Hamish and Vanessa's interior is not just, or not only, an original expression of their personalities (it is that as well) but also follows fashion. Hamish and Vanessa not only use the meaning potentials of colour differentiation and saturation to express their personalities, they also draw on cultural connotations, and thereby on the values of the 'place' (in this case the period, the eighteenth and nineteenth centuries) where these colours come from. By decorating their home with these colours, do they symbolically identify with the values of a past era, and with the nostalgia for a 'lost' Englishness that was so salient throughout the 1990s? Perhaps. But neither they nor the author of the article say so.

To sum up:

- In relation to lifestyle identity, the meanings of colours are unstable. They can be made and remade. They are disposable and replaceable.

- Colour might signify either or both of two kinds of lifestyle meaning – personality traits, or the values connoted by the place or time from which they are derived, and, although both continue to exist alongside of each other, it would appear that the principle of connotation and 'composite of connotation' is taking over from the principle of individual personality – 'wild', for instance, is no longer an individual character trait, but a quality of an environment (e.g. the 'corporate jungle') that can then be evoked by a colour ('wild animal prints will help you look the part in the corporate jungle').

- In lifestyle media, colour meanings are interpreted as 'always new' and as a creation of the sign producer:

> There are certain accessories that signify change, that identify new territory. Find them and you've found the fastest, easiest way to transform the look of any garment, no matter what its price tag.
>
> (*Australian Vogue*, November 1997: 220)

- People are not necessarily consciously aware of all the connotations of the colours they use. They might, for instance, wear military colours without intending to convey any form of identification with the military. If asked why they wear these colours, they might say, 'I wear them because they are cool', 'I wear them because I like them', etc. Yet the military connotation is objectively there. The military is objectively the 'place where this colour comes from'. Appeals to fashion and taste can disavow meaning, and allow people to take distance from the very things they are signifying.

- Normative discourses can take many different forms – rules, advice, suggestions, guidelines, and so on. There is reason to think that 'role model' discourses are in the ascendance, also in fashion. Magazines increasingly use established or up-and-coming celebrities to profile the latest fashions, and fashion models have become less anonymous. The singular dictate of fashion that Roland Barthes wrote about might, in the age of consumer choice, make place for choice between a *range* of trends ('the *five* trends you'll be wearing this season'), and a *range* of role models. In the matter of lifestyle identity, choice – or the illusion of choice – is all important.

In this identity function, colour is rapidly becoming a global medium. The consumer goods that form the major semiotic resource for the expression of lifestyles are globally distributed. The meanings associated with their colours are elaborated in texts and practices used in design schools across the world and popularized in globally distributed media. As a result the same lifestyles and the same colours can be recognized across the world, in the streets of Boston as well as Barcelona, Sydney as well as Shanghai, Tokyo as well as Toronto.

7.3 Textuality

A second important contemporary use of colour is textuality. As mentioned in Chapter 2, colour has re-entered the 'monochrome' world of texts, and not just in the form of illustrations. The *structure* of texts in magazines, websites and other modern media is now often signalled, not by means of words, but by means of layout, colour and typograpy, so much so that without layout, colour and typography, many of these texts would be incomprehensible. Without the differently coloured boxes, and the way in which they are distributed across the page, the words on the web page shown in Figure 7.2 would read something like this:

> Font merchandise LetterSetter Free Catalog News Licensing Tech Support Contact custom work Free Fonts Search Find it Jump to font kit Try fonts before you buy with LetterSetter Strike! House-a-Rama Font Kit $ 100 Three Fonts 54 Dingbats 14 Illustrations Four patterns Buy it Now! House-a-Rama $ 100 View fonts View Font Specimens View Illustrations View Patterns & Dingbats Try Fonts with LetterSetter House-a-Rama Buy it Now!

Clearly, in this kind of writing, things, people, places, activities etc. are, for the most part, still communicated verbally (with the exception of the Font Kit bag in the centre), but the *connection* between the words is now visual. The textual coherence that ultimately allows the words to make sense is created by layout, colour and typography. This kind of writing mixes the visual and the verbal in new ways, and, as a result, can no longer be meaningfully read aloud, breaking the age-old connection between spoken and written language. In this context, colour has three specific textual functions:

- Colour can help segment the text into various meaningful units by creating *framings* (see Van Leeuwen, 2005: 6–24) identified by distinct colours. In Figure 7.2, for instance, local navigation (left column) is black, branding and global navigation (top) a slightly greenish grey, and specific content (centre) white. While providing framing, these colours can, of course, at the same time, signify brand identity – 'identity' and the 'textuality' operate *simultaneously* and are not mutually exclusive.

- Colour can provide *salience* and help draw attention to elements that are considered particularly important. In Figure 7.2 the red colour stands out, drawing attention to the 'font kit' in the centre.

- Colour can provide overall cohesion. If, in a PowerPoint presentation, a background colour is chosen, this colour usually remains constant across all slides, thus creating a sense of unity, while at the same time expressing 'identity', whether the identity of the speaker or that of the genre of presentation. A chief accountant at a university presented the university's annual budget figures against a pale blue background in which the outlines of a calm blue ocean and sky could only just be discerned. He also inserted some quotations from business gurus between the slides presenting the budget figures. Clearly, he wanted to present himself as a man with strategic vision, rather than just an accountant. Such identities may be personal or corporate.

- Colour identity can also express genre (a children's website might use saturated primary colour, for instance) or relate to the subject matter. I once gave a PowerPoint-supported talk about perfumes, linking the visual qualities of perfume ads to the actual smell of the advertised perfumes – and using a salmon pink coloured background to underline the sensuality of smell.

In website design, cascading style sheets are used to give sites an integrated, 'uniform appearance' (Smith, 2005: 158), allowing a single external file to dictate the colour and typography of every page of the site.

Figure 7.3 shows the layout, typography and colour of an insert in an article in *Cosmopolitan magazine* (November 2004: 18) – we were not allowed to reproduce the original article.

The photograph at the top shows a young man smiling at the viewer, with the text (top left) 'You're gonna have to dig'. The photo challenges the female readers of the magazine: 'Don't think you can know me at first sight. You will have to dig deeper'. The headline, in white, then announces that the text will reveal 'Things You Only Learn With Time', and the sub-headline adds, 'Your speedy profiling skills won't reveal these tidbits'. This is followed by four of the things that are 'inside his head' and can only be 'learnt with time', each headlined in white: 'How loyal he'll be', 'If he's a man of his word', 'His little quirks', and 'If his parents' split haunts him'. The text underneath each of these headlines elaborates the point further, e.g. under 'His little quirks', we read 'Time reveals the small details that really make a person tick'. In a traditional text, this structure would be indicated verbally ('there are four things about men you can only learn with time . . .'; 'Firstly, how loyal he will be', 'Secondly, if he's man of his word', and so on) and with conventional typographic means – font size, spacing between lines, indentation. But here colour is the key. It sets apart the three kinds of structural element from which the text is built up: (1) the *background*, which expresses the identity of the text – a contemplative blue; (2) the headings, which summarize the content of the text as a whole and the content of the sections – white; and (3) the copy – black. These colours, together with the contrast between the photo and the rest of the text, show in a split second how the article is structured: A *problem* (how to really know your man, as expressed by the photograph and its accompanying text) and its *solution* (the rest of the article), and, within the solution, first the *key* to the solution (focus on 'Things You Only Learn With Time') and then four specific *'tips'*.

The visual 'format' of this text is not unique to this particular example. In a study of 48 different versions of *Cosmopolitan* magazine, Machin and Van Leeuwen (2007) found that the content of versions produced in different countries differs, even though all focus on the same agenda of beauty, health, careers, relationships and sex. But visually they look very much the same, all adopting this kind of 'hot tips' format. Even in countries without a *Cosmopolitan* franchise, such as Vietnam, editors of local women's magazines use *Cosmopolitan* as their model because, as the editor of a Vietnamese women's magazine said, 'advertisers favour this kind of style:' (*ibid.*: 58). As Machin and Van Leeuwen commented (*ibid.*: 170):

> Visual discourses are increasingly global, designed to fit in with the layout of adver- tisements and other global messages, and focusing on the symbolic representation of the values and identities of late capitalist consumer society. It is also visually, through self- presentation (dress and other lifestyle attributes) that people can recognize others as belonging to the same dispersed lifestyle or taste communities.

Figure 7.4 is a page from a textbook for clinicians about the physical examination and 'history taking' of patients (Bickley, 2009). To understand the textual function of colour on this page (and in the textbook as a whole), first consider the difference between the text in the pale grey-green box and the text below it. The former contains questions about pain in any area of the body (for instance, 'determine whether the pain is *localized* or *diffuse*, *acute* or *chronic*, *inflammatory* or *noninflammatory*'), the latter questions about pain in specific parts of the body, as indicated by the blue headlines ('Low Back Pain', 'Neck Pain', etc.). Then there is the difference between the black-lettered column on the left and the red-lettered column on the right. The left column contains questions, the right column notes on the possible or likely answers to these questions (which can then be used to formulate further questions or to diagnose the problem). Again, colour *marks* different textual elements of the text which in traditional texts would be linked verbally.

Not only magazines and textbooks, but newspapers also have become more visual. In an article documenting the redesign of the English-language *South China Morning Post*, designer James de Vries (2008) describes the fundamental role of layout, colour and typography in integrating the complex and diverse content of newspapers into a clear and easily navigable structure.

As can be seen in Figure 7.5, the *South China Morning Post* palette first of all frames the different sections of the newspaper. As De Vries recounts, deciding on these 'theme colours' took some time (2008: 21):

We were trying to get a good spread across the spectrum, but our client preferred red. So we ended up using three different reds: the sport section red, the city section red, and a main news red. We proposed a crimsony red for their lifestyle sections (which has a lot of material about shopping, beauty, etc.). But this met with resistance from the management committee. They thought it was too feminine and a bit 'tarty' – there was a specific Chinese word for that. In the end we prevailed, though it was in fact our second approach. We had first proposed an eggy yellowy colour which they had absolutely rejected.

Red has long been a key colour for the masthead of, especially, tabloid papers, perhaps signifying that news is 'hot', and red, white and black have signalled the identity of many news magazines. But more recently, led by the much discussed redesign of *The Guardian*, blue has become more important, especially in the case of business news but, in many papers, also elsewhere. At the same time, violets and purples have come into use in 'softer' sections, e.g. lifestyle sections, although clearly the *South China Morning Post* was not quite ready for this. The colour palette of newspapers thus betrays a mixed identity – the red excitement of news and sport, the calm and steely blue of business, and the more 'impure' and sensuous violets and purples of lifestyle sections.

Within each section, there is a choice either between different values of the same colour, as in the case of the business section of the *South China Morning Post*, with its various values of blue, and/or combining the 'thematic' colour with the 'daily jades' shown on the left of the palette. These different shades have textual functions within the individual pages, rather than within the newspaper as a whole. The 'theme' colour itself is used for section headings, and for certain kinds of page furniture, such as the logos and banners that may head columns or articles or refer to web information or feedback options, while the lighter colours or jades are used to frame boxes, sidebars, etc. De Vries advocates no more than three or four levels of salience (2008: 19, 21):

> There might be ten articles, but there is no point in ranking them one to ten, I believe readers want to be told what is the most important, the next most important, and from then on they will work it out for themselves . . . Colour is a very powerful tool, but it is easy for designers to overdo colour and develop multilevel colour symbolisms that are completely irrelevant to readers. As a function of our short-term memories, a system of three or four colour-coded themes is about all most readers can take meaning from. The rest is subconscious.

Modern writing software such as Word, HTML, and PowerPoint allows users to colour their writing, and has brought colour into previously monochrome text types such as typed reports and lecture overhead slides. Such software might come with built-in ideas about what colour is (e.g. what parameters it contains) and how it should be used. In PowerPoint, colour schemes can either be preset or constructed by the user – according to certain rules, and in a certain order. First, a background colour is chosen, then a colour for the text and the title of the slide, then one or two colours for 'fills' (e.g. the bars of bar graphs), and finally one or two colours for 'accents' (e.g. bullet points or hyperlinks). A colour for shadows can also be chosen.

The background colour plays a key role in conveying the identity of the presenter or the presentation, and can be freely chosen. In early PowerPoint versions, only hue, value and saturation could be manipulated, but later modulation became possible as well (by means of 'gradients', 'patterns' and 'textures'). Given a certain background colour, there are restrictions on the colour of the title and the text, as they must be legible against the background – dark when the background is light, and light when the background is dark, for instance. Accents need to stand out even more, and shadows must contrast with both background and text. A typical colour scheme might look like this:

Background: relatively dark blue-grey
Text and lines: white
Title: yellow
Shadows: black
Fills: orange
Accent 1:   red
Accent 2:   turquoise

Users can either pick colours from a Munsell chart or mix colours themselves, using slides to vary the amount of red, green and blue in each colour, and to adjust their value and saturation. These colours can then be imported into any of the functional 'slots' (i.e. 'Background', 'Text and lines', etc.).

In PowerPoint 2007, colour schemes changed in two fundamental ways. The functional schema was extended to 12 functions: Background 1, Background 2, Text 1, Text 2, six different Accents, Hyperlink and Followed hyperlink, and the preset schemes were given names not unlike those of the colour schemes by Le Corbusier discussed in Chapter 6 – names such as 'Office', 'Civic', 'Flow', 'Metro', 'Opulent', 'Technic', 'Urban', 'Verve'. 'Verve', for instance, has predominantly blues and violets of different degrees of saturation and value, two greys, and white and black. White, grey and black dominate text and background, blues and violets are used for accents and hyperlinks, in what is overall a rather cold and artificial-looking scheme, combining business-like blue-grey with a pale, ice lolly violet. 'Foundry' combines a wider range of colours, almost all pale and pastel (soft pink, soft yellow, pale blue, pale green, off-white) except for a somewhat more saturated olive accent colour.

In other words, PowerPoint *builds in* what I have identified as the two key contemporary functions of colour:

• The function of providing overall cohesion, 'colour-marking' the functional elements of each slide (the title and the bullet points, for instance) and providing extra salience to elements that are deemed particularly important (e.g. hyperlinks).

• The function of providing 'identity' for the whole of the presentation, through colour schemes whose parametric composition foregrounds particular values, and through the possibility of adding expressive texture to the background.

Like other semiotic softwares, PowerPoint therefore also builds in a normative discourse, a system for regulating what colour *is* (e.g. what parameters can be realized) and how it should be used, the latter enforced through the order of items on menus, default choices, built-in preferences, and so on. Of course, in a way 'enforced' is too strong a word. People can make their own rules, if they want to. Yet most people don't and most PowerPoint lectures, business presentations and so on look pretty alike, whether because it is easiest to follow the road of least resistance, or because of the conformity of practice that tends to come about wherever no clear-cut rules exist. Ellen Lupton (2004: 135) said that 'We do have a language of vision now, but it was created by corporate software developers'. Likewise we can say that, through tools such as PowerPoint, Dreamweaver, Photoshop, and so on, 'We do have a language of colour now, but it was created by corporate software developers'.

7.4 Conclusion

To end, let me try to draw a few key points together.

- There have been some significant turnarounds in the role of colour in cultural expression and social communication. In medieval times, colour was highly valued for its intrinsic, material qualities, its brilliance and its lustre, and signified key identities and key values and ideas. A more monochrome age followed. In everyday life, colour gave way to Puritan neutrality and black. Artists began to use it naturalistically rather than symbolically. Theorists studied it scientifically rather than semiotically. In the twentieth century, colour re-entered many of the domains from which it had earlier retreated, and its material qualities began to be appreciated again. But the extent of this breakthrough has varied with fashion, and periods of festive, sparkling colour have alternated with returns to more neutral colour, enlivened, at best, with modest splashes of more lively colour.

- There has never been a single language of colour. Colour codes with a restricted semantic reach have always proliferated, and sometimes contradicted each other. But there are also broader, longer lasting, and more widely distributed trends, such as the reign of 'puritan black' or the ascendance of blue which Pastoureau has so excellently documented (2001, 2008).

- Semiotically, colour has always been able to convey ideational, interpersonal and textual meanings, but at certain times and in certain periods one or other of these functions has dominated over others, in the practice of using colour as well as in colour discourses. Today, emotive, psychological colour meanings continue to play a role, but, alongside of this, two other uses and two other discourses of colour have come into ascendance: colour in the service of textual structure, with its affinity to grammar, and its tendency to system building, especially in the context of computer applications; and lifestyle identity colour, often inspired by a wide and eclectic range of references to cultural history – designers continue to prefer case studies of the '100 ideas for colour combinations' variety over more systematic accounts.

- New colour meanings can be based on the meaning potentials of the kinds of colour parameters discussed in Chapter 5, but there are no hard and fast rules, no algorithms, for determining just how much and what kind of weight each parameter puts in the scale. Both the creation and the interpretation of such meanings remain an art form, and Josef Albers' observation still applies (1975: 42):

  > Good colouring is comparable to good cooking. Even a good cooking recipe demands tasting and repeated tasting while it is being followed. And the best tasting still depends on a cook with taste.

  Similarly, the best interpretation demands repeated, continuous checking of one's intuitions on ever new examples – and the best interpretations still depend on an interpreter with wide experience and a wide range of references to draw on.

- Colour schemes have gradually become a more important source of colour meaning than individual colours, taking their meaning from the *relations* between colours, and grafting oppositions of meaning or textual function onto oppositions between the parameters of the colours in the scheme.

For some centuries now, there has been a mismatch between a colour theory based on physical facts and a colour theory based on psychological effects. The two theories, the scientific theory of colour form and the psychological theory of colour meaning, do not easily fit and theorists and artists alike have struggled with this problem. Semiotically, too, colour pulls us in two directions: on the one hand moving towards systematicity, towards the status of a mode; on the other hand, exploring the material affordances of colour and returning to colour as medium. Semioticians might be pulled in the direction of systematicity. That is their bent and their strength. But *social* semioticians must account for colour as it is actually used in society, in all its complexities, and with all its contradictions.

Exercises

1   In the following fragment from *The System of Objects* (1996), Jean Baudrillard relates the ascendance of the 'colour scheme' to what he sees as an increasingly functional approach to colour. How does this functional approach differ from previous approaches, according to Baudrillard, and what does he see as its main characteristics?

> After a few brief episodes of violent liberation (notably in the world of art, with, in the end, but mild impact upon everyday life – except of course for the spheres of advertising and commerce, where colour enjoys full rein), colour was immediately taken back in hand by a system in *which nature no longer plays any part except as naturalness* – as a mere connotation of nature behind whose screen instinctual values continue to be subtly disavowed. Nevertheless, the very abstractness of these now 'free' colours means that they are at last able to play an active role. It is towards this third stage that colour is at present orientating itself . . . Indeed in a sense we are no longer dealing with colours *per se* but with more abstract values. The combination, matching and contrast of tones are the real issues . . . Blue can go with green – all colours are capable of combination – but only certain blues with certain greens; furthermore it is not so much a question of blue and green as of *hot and cold*. At the same time, colour is no longer a way of emphasizing each object by setting it off from the décor; colours are now contrasting ranges of shades, their value has less and less to do with their sensory qualities, they are often dissociated from their form, and it is their tonal difference that give a room its 'rhythm'. Just as modular furniture loses its specific functions so much that at the logical extreme its value resides solely in the positioning of each movable element, so likewise colours lose their unique value, and become relative to each other and to the whole. This is what is meant by describing them, as 'functional'.

> Consider the following description from a practical guide to interior decoration:

> . . .

> A plain matte white background interrupted by great blue surfaces (on the ceiling). White and blue repeated in the arrangement of the décor: a white marble table, a screen partition . . . A warm touch is supplied by the bright red doors of a low

storage unit. In fact we find ourselves in a space handled entirely in plain colours, devoid of any nuances of tone or of any softness (all the softness having taken refuge in the picture on the left), albeit balanced by large areas of white.

Here is another example: 'The little indoor tropical garden is not just protected but also lent rhythm by a slab of black enameled glass'. (Notice that black and white in these descriptions retain nothing of their traditional value; they have escaped from the white-black polarity and taken on a *tactical v*alue within the extended range of all colours. . . . Once again, this is what makes a colour 'functional' – that is to say, reduced to an abstract conceptual element of calculation.

2 Compare the colours of Meccano, traditional Lego blocks, and the Lego blocks in boxes for building specific models (e.g. Star Wars space vehicles). What are the meanings or meaning potentials of each, and what are they motivated by?

3 Choose a fairly short traditional 'linear' text (e.g. an article from a print encyclopaedia) and rewrite it, using colour and layout to distinguish particular text elements (e.g. 'definition', 'historical background', 'sub-types' of whatever the subject of the article is, 'examples', etc.).

Notes

1 Introduction

1   The section that follows is a revised version of part of Kress and van Leeuwen, 2002.

2 Colour meanings

1   Especially in heraldry, tinctures were often associated with precious stones. There were different views on which colours corresponded to which gemstones. Diamond was sometimes associated with black, sometimes with blue.

7 Colour in contemporary life

1   The first two sections of this chapter draw on sections from Van Leeuwen, 2005, chapter 3.
2   This section relies on research by Emilia Djonov, conducted as part of a joint, ARC-funded research project on the semiotics of PowerPoint.

Glossary

Abstract modality

A criterion for judging the *modality* of a *sign* or set of signs, e.g. a colour or *colour scheme*. In abstract modality, truth is cognitive truth: the more the colour of an object represents what is regarded as the essential colour of that object (e.g. the green of grass, or the blue of water), rather than what the object might look like at specific times of day, or under specific light conditions, the higher its abstract modality.

Achromatic grey

See *Saturation*.

Additive colour mixing

The mixing of coloured light. The additive primaries are red, green and blue. When green, blue and red light is mixed together in equal proportions, white light results.

Adjacent colours

Colours that are adjacent on a *colour wheel*.

Affordance

Affordances (Gibson, 1979) are the potential uses of a given object, stemming from the perceivable properties of the object. Because perception is selective, depending on the needs and interest of the perceivers, different perceivers will notice different affordances. But those that remain unnoticed continue to exist objectively, latent in the object, waiting to be discovered.

Afterimage

An optical illusion that makes a colour's *complementary* appear. When a coloured circle is looked at intently for 20 seconds, the complementary appears as a halo around the circle, or, after closing the eyes, as a mental image.

Arbitrary

The relation between a *signifier* and a *signified* is arbitrary when there is no apparent reason (*motivation*) for that particular signifier to signify that particular signified, e.g. the colours of the lines on a railway system map.

Attribute

See *Symbolic attribute*.

Brightness

A synonym for *value*.

Carrier

A person, place or thing whose meaning or identity is established by a *symbolic attribute*.

Chiaroscuro
Italian for 'dark light'. The use of shadow and light to create the illusion of three-dimensional space on a flat surface (and sometimes to create a dramatic effect).

Chromatic grey
See *Saturation*

Colour harmony
See *Colour scheme*

Colour scheme
A palette of colours designed for a particular kind of application, and selected according to explicit criteria, e.g. four *values* of each of two *complementary colours*.

Colour wheel
A circular arrangement of colours and their relationships used to visualize a theory of colour. It might show only *primary* and *secondary colours*, or also *tertiary colours*. *Complementary colours* are placed opposite each other. Colours of different *value* or *saturation* may be shown in concentric circles.

Complementary colours
Colours that are opposite each other on a *colour wheel*. Complementary colours include the primary or primaries that are not included in the colours they are the complementaries of. For instance, the complementary colour of the primary colour red is green, the mixture of the other two primaries (blue and yellow), and the complementary colour of purple, which mixes blue and red, is yellow, the primary colour that is not included in purple itself.

Composite of connotation
A composite of *connotation* fuses a number of connotative signs of different *provenance*. For instance, a writing style might combine elements from the style of advertising with elements from the style of casual conversation to connote informality as well as allegiance to consumer values and designer taste. Composites of connotation are particularly favoured in signifying *lifestyle identity*.

Connotation
Connotation is based on *provenance*, on 'where things come from'. It occurs when a *semiotic resource* (e.g. the colour pink) is imported from one domain into another where it is not normally used (e.g. motor cars). It then stands for the ideas and values which those who import the resource associate with the domain from which they have imported it (e.g. femininity in the case of pink). Connotative *signs* generally signify ideas and values rather than referring to concrete, specific people, places and things.

Content
In the linguistics of Hjelmslev, language fuses two main layers, or 'strata'. The stratum of 'content' organizes content by means of the lexicon and the grammar of language. The stratum of 'expression' organizes the expression matter, which could either be speech or writing. Kress and Van Leeuwen have reformulated this for the purposes of *social semiotics*, as *design* and *production*.

CYMK
Abbreviation of cyan, yellow, magenta, key (black); the four colours used in colour printing.

Design
Designs, in the sense in which this term is used in *social semiotics* (Kress and Van Leeuwen, 2001) are conceptualizations of semiotic artefacts and events, which can take the form of a 'script', a 'score', 'a blue-print', 'a sketch', or only exist in the mind of the designer. Three things are designed simultaneously: a particular organization of the content, a particular (inter)action in which this content is embedded, and a particular way of using semiotic resources. *Production* then gives designs their material, perceivable form.

Differentiation
The number of different colours in a visual object or colour scheme, ranging from monochrome to a maximally diverse palette of colours.

Disguised symbolism
See *Symbolism*.

Distinctive features
Distinctive features (Jakobson and Halle, 1956) are the qualities of speech sounds that serve to differentiate the speech sounds in the sound system of a language from each other, e.g. voiced/voiceless, strident/mellow, tense/lax.

Experiential metaphor
A metaphor understands one thing in terms of another thing with which it has a relation of (partial) similarity. According to Lakoff and Johnson (1980) our understanding of the world is based on metaphors. In this way we are able to understand complex and abstract ideas on the basis of concrete experiences. In *social semiotics*, experiential metaphor is one of the ways in which a *sign* can be motivated, for instance by the concrete qualities of the *signifier* (the lustre of silver or the darkness of black), or by the way it is physically produced (for instance, the texture of rusty iron).

Expression
Expression, in the linguistics of Hjelmslev, is the signifying layer of language which organizes perceivable actions (e.g. speech sounds) or substances (e.g. letter forms on paper) in order to enable them to express *content*.

Framing
Framing creates a sense of disconnection or separateness between the elements of a composition or layout, for instance by means of frame lines, empty space, or discontinuities of various kinds, including differently coloured backgrounds, for instance in text boxes.
The concept also includes the creation of a sense of connection between the elements of a semiotic artefact or event, for instance through the absence of framing devices or by means of similarity between the elements (for instance, similarity of colour).
The significance of this is that disconnected elements will be understood as in some sense separate and independent, perhaps even contrasting, while connected elements will be understood as in some sense belonging together.

High key
An image is said to be high key when its colours are predominantly light.

Hue
Term for the actual chromatic quality of a colour (its redness, greenness, etc.), as opposed to its *value* or *saturation*.

Ideational function
M.A.K. Halliday's term for the semiotic *metafunction* of constructing representations of what is going on in the world.

Identity
The identity of a person comprises the attributes by means of which he or she (or some other person or institution) indicates who s/he is in a given context. *Individual identity* is the unique identity of a person, seen as capturing his or her enduring character and personality. *Social identity* indexes the categories which define shared identities in a given social or institutional context, such as provenance, gender, class, procession, etc. *Lifestyle identity* is defined by individual lifestyle choices (especially leisure time activities, attitudes to contemporary issues and consumer choices) which are, however, socially produced and shared with others.

Individual identity
See *Identity*.

Interpersonal function
M.A.K. Halliday's term for the semiotic *metafunction* of constituting communicative interactions.

Iridescence
Iridescence creates a shimmer of different colours. It results from movement, making objects seem to glitter as their movement, or the movement of the viewer, causes changes in the viewer's angle of vision.

Lifestyle identity
See *Identity*.

Low key
An image is said to be low key when its colours are predominantly dark.

Luminescence
Luminescent colours glow because they are lit from behind (e.g. stained glass, coloured neon light) or because they are themselves a source of light (e.g. burning coal).

Luminosity
Luminous ('brilliant') colours give an impression of glow that seems to come from an inherent light.

Lustre
The sheen or gloss of a colour deriving from the reflectivity of the coloured surface.

Meaning potential
The kinds of meanings that have been associated with a particular object or quality of an object in a given cultural context.

Medium
Media are the material resources used in the production of communicative artefacts and events. They produce meaning through the processes of *connotation* and *experiential metaphor*.

Metafunctions
The broad communicative functions of language, and, by extension, other modes of communication, including colour.

Modality
A set of *semiotic resources* for indicating the truth of semiotic means of expression, including colour. *Naturalistic modality*, *abstract modality*, and *sensory modality* are based on different truth criteria.

Modulation
Colour modulation is the scale that runs from flat colour to a maximally nuanced colour, e.g. from grass as plain green, to grass represented with a range of shades and tints (Degas once proposed a series of still-lives of loaves of bread showing the 'yellows, pinks, greys and whites of bread' (Riley, 1995: 79).

Motivation
The relation between a *signifier* and a *signified* is motivated when we can see a reason why a particular signifier signifies a particular signified, e.g. gold as a signifier of value.

Naturalistic modality
This term is used in *social semiotics* for one of the criteria for judging the *modality* of a *sign*, e.g. a colour. In naturalistic modality truth is 'perceptual' truth: the more the colour of a represented object or landscape looks like the colour we would have seen if we had seen that object or landscape in reality, under specific light conditions, the higher its naturalistic modality.

Normative discourses
Discourses that regulate how *semiotic resources* should be used in particular contexts, whether in formal or informal ways, and whether prescriptively and authoritatively or by means of suggestion and advice.

Open symbolism
See *Symbolism*.

PMS
Abbrevation of 'Pantone Matching System', a system of recipes for printers that specify the proportions of cyan, yellow, magenta and black needed to produce specific colours.

Primary colour
Strictly, primary colours are colours that cannot be obtained by mixing red, blue and yellow in the case of *subtractive mixing*, and red, green and blue in the case of *additive mixing*. More broadly, they are colours (usually up to seven, depending on the theorist you follow) regarded as fundamental and irreducible in the context of some system of classification.

Production
Production, in the sense in which the term is used in *social semiotics* (Kress and Van Leeuwen, 2001) is the articulation in material form of semiotic products or events. Production not only gives perceivable form to designs, but also adds meanings that may either rely on *connotation* or flow directly from the

physical process of articulation and the physical qualities of the materials used, by means of the process of *experiential metaphor*.

Proportion

Colour proportionality refers to the amount to which each of the colours of a colour scheme is used in that scheme. It can be represented by means of a 'proportional colour inventory' (Hornung, 2005).

Provenance

The provenance of something is its 'origin', the place where it comes from. In *social semiotics* the term is often used synonymously with *connotation*.

Purity

Strictly speaking, pure colours are *primary colours*, colours which, objectively, cannot be obtained by mixing. More broadly, they are colours which, subjectively, are perceived as irreducible, rather than as some combination of other colours, e.g. green might not be experienced as a combination of blue and yellow, but blue-green will most likely be experienced as a combination of blue and green.

Salience

Salience creates difference between the elements of a composition in terms of the degree to which they attract the viewer's attention. It can be achieved by movement (in an environment where other things do not move), relative size, relative amount of detail and texture shown, contrasts of hue, value or saturation, placement in the visual field and specific cultural factors such as the appearance of the human figure.

Saturation

Saturation is the degree of purity of a colour. Different degrees of saturation are best imagined as degrees to which grey (or a complementary colour) is mixed in with a colour, keeping it equally light or dark, but gradually more muted, until it becomes a 'chromatic grey', a grey in which a tinge of colour can only just be detected, and, finally, an 'achromatic', colourless grey.

Secondary colour

A colour mixed from two *primary colours*. The *additive* secondaries are cyan, magenta and yellow. The *subtractive* secondaries are purple, orange and green.

Semiotic resources

Semiotic resources are the actions, materials and artefacts people use for cultural expression and social communication, whether produced physiologically (e.g. speaking or gesturing) or technologically (e.g. pen and ink, computer software), together with the way they have been organized or adapted for purposes of communication and expression.

Sensory modality

A criterion for judging the *modality* of a *sign*, e.g. a colour, which rests on the colour's ability to arouse an affective response of pleasure or displeasure. The stronger this response, the higher the modality.

Shade

The result of mixing a colour with black.

Sign

An instance of the use of a *semiotic resource* for purposes of communication, for instance the action of frowning for communicating disapproval, or the use of red for warning against some danger.

Signified

The meaning we express with a *signifier*, for example 'disapproval' in the case of a frown, and 'danger' in the case of a red sign.

Signifier

The observable form we use to communicate, for instance a facial expression or a colour.

Social identity

See *Identity*.

Social semiotics

The study of the way *semiotic resources* are organized and used, both generally, and in specific social, cultural and historical contexts.

Subtractive colour mixing

The mixing of colouring agents such as paints, dyes and inks. The subtractive primaries are red, yellow and blue. When all three are mixed together, (a muddy) black results.

Symbolic attribute

An element or quality in a representation that serves to signify the meaning or identity of some other element in terms of specific values and ideas.

Symbolism

A semiotic process in which a *symbolic attribute* relates a *carrier* to specific values and ideas in order to communicate what the meaning or identity of the carrier is in the given context.

Temperature

Colours at the red end of the spectrum are said to be 'warm', colours on the blue end of the spectrum 'cold'.

Tertiary colour

Tertiary colours result from mixing *primary* and *secondary colours*, e.g. yellow-orange, orange-red, etc.

Textual function

M.A.K. Halliday's term for the *metafunction* of creating texts, complexes of signs which cohere both internally with each other and externally with the context in and for which they are produced.

Texture

A term for the tactile qualities of coloured surfaces (e.g. their roughness or smoothness). It is often extended to refer also to patterns that cannot be sensed by touch, for instances the veining of marble, or the grain of wood.

Tint

The result of mixing a colour with white.

Translucency

Translucent colours allow partial visibility of what lies behind them, while at the same time softening and diffusing the objects behind them.

Transparency

Transparent colours allow visibility of what lies behind them.

Value

The relative lightness or darkness of a colour.

References

Albers, J. (1975[1963]) *Interaction of Colour*, New Haven, CT: Yale University Press

Appolonio, U. (ed.) (2009) *Futurist Manifestos*, London: Tate Publishing

Archer, A. (in press) 'Red socks and purple rain: the political uses of colour in late apartheid South Africa', *Visual Communication*

Aristotle (1954) *The Rhetoric and the Poetics*, New York: Random House

Arnheim, R. (1974) *Art and Visual Perception – a psychology of the creative eye*, Berkeley and Los Angeles: University of California Press

Barthes, R. (1983) *The Fashion System*, Berkeley and Los Angeles: University of California Press

Batchelor, D. (2000) *Chromophobia*, London: Reaktion Books

Baudrillard, J. (1996) *The System of Objects*, London: Verso

Benjamin, A. (1989) *The Lyotard Reader*, Oxford: Oxford University Press

Berlin, B. and Kay, P. (1991) *Basic Color Terms – their universality and evolution*, 2nd edition, Berkeley: University of California Press

Bickley, L.S. (2009) *Pocket Guide to Physical Examination and History Taking*, Philadelphia: Wolters Kluwer

Birren, F. (1961) *Color Psychology and Color Therapy*, Secaucus, NJ: University Books

Bogatyrev, P. (1971[1937]) *The Function of Folk Costume in Moravian Slovakia*, The Hague: Mouton

Bolinger, D. (1972) 'Around the Edge of Language: Intonation', in D. Bolinger (ed.) *Intonation*, Harmondsworth: Penguin

Chaney, D. (1996) *Lifestyles*, London: Routledge

Coca-Cola (2010) http://questions.coca-cola.com/NSREExtended.asp?WhatUserSaid=coca-cola+red&VRepTalk.x=12&VRepTalk.y=15 (accessed 12 February 2010)

Cole, D. (2007) *Patterns – New Surface Design*, London: Laurence King

Completecraft (2010) www.completecraft.com.au/articles

Conklin, H. (1964) 'Hanuhóo Colour Categories', in Dell H. Hymes (ed.) *Language in Culture and Society*, New York, Harper Row

Crystal, C. (1975) *The English Tone of Voice*, London: Arnold

Da Vinci, L. (2005) *Leonardo's Notebooks*, New York: Blackdog & Leventhal Publishers

De Heer, J. (2008) *De architectonische kleur – De polychromie in de puristische architectuur van Le Corbusier*, Rotterdam: Uitgeverij 010

De Vries, J. (2008) 'Newspaper design as cultural change', *Visual Communication* 7(1): 5–27

Derrida, J. (1987) *The Truth in Painting*, Chicago: Chicago University Press

Djonov, E. and Van Leeuwen, T. (in press) 'The Semiotics of Texture According to PowerPoint', *Visual Communication*

Eco, U. (ed.) (2002) *History of Beauty*, New York: Rizzoli

Feisner, E.A. (2006) *Colour – how to use colour in art and design*, 2nd edition, London: Laurence King

Fiedler, J. (ed.) (2006) *Bauhaus*, Berlin: Könemann

Finlay, V. (2002) *Colour – travels through the paintbox*, London: Hodder and Stoughton

Fischer, E.P. (1996) *Color Systems in Art and Science*, Konstanz: Regenbogen Verlag

Gage, J. (1993) *Colour and Culture – practice and meaning from antiquity to abstraction*, London: Thames and Hudson

Gage, J. (1999) *Colour and Meaning – art, science and symbolism*, London: Thames and Hudson

Gibson, J.J. (1979) *The Ecological Approach to Visual Perception*, Boston, MA: Houghton Mifflin

Goethe, J.W. von (1970[1812]) *Theory of Colours*, Cambridge, MA: MIT Press

Goodman, S. and Graddol, D. (1996) *Redesigning English: new texts, new identities*, London: Routledge

Halliday, M.A.K. (1978) *Language as Social Semiotic*, London: Arnold

Heeschen, V. (2006) 'Attractiveness and Adornment', in M. Plümacher and P. Holz (eds) *Speaking of Colors and Odors*, Amsterdam: John Benjamins, pp. 85–111

Hegel, G.W.F. (1975) *Aesthetics – lectures on fine art*, Oxford: Clarendon Press

Hermeren, G. (1969) *Representation and Meaning in the Visual Arts*, Lund: Scandinavian University Books

Hornung, D. (2005) *Colour – a workshop for artists and designers*, London: Laurence King

HSBC (2006) *HSBC Brand Basic Elements Group Marketing*, June 2006

Hunter, L. (2006) 'Critical form as everyday practice – an interview with Ellen Lupton', *Information Design Journal* 14(2): 130–8

Huxtable, M.J. (2006) 'The Medieval Gaze at Grips with the Medieval World', in C.P. Biggam and C.J. Kay (eds) *Progress in Colour Studies, Volume I, Language and Culture*, Amsterdam: John Benjamins, pp. 199–217

Itten, J. (1970) *The Elements of Color*, New York: Van Nostrand Reinhold

Jaffé, H.L.C. (1967) *De Stijl*, New York: Harry N. Abrams, Inc.

Jakobson, R. (1960) 'Closing Statement: Linguistics and Poetics', in T.A. Sebeok (ed.) *Style in Language*, Cambridge, MA: MIT Press

Jakobson, R. and Halle, M. (1956) 'Phonology in Relation to Phonetics', in B. Malmberg (ed.) *Manual of Phonetics*, Amsterdam: North Holland

Jakobson, R. and Halle, M. (1973) 'Distinctive Features', in E. Fudge (ed.) *Phonology*, Harmondsworth: Penguin, pp. 151–9

Jennings, S. (2008) *Collins Artist's Little Book of Colour*, London: HarperCollins Publishers

Kandinsky, W. (1977[1914]) *Concerning the Spiritual in Art*, New York: Dover Publications

Kant, I. (1978[1790]) *The Critique of Judgement*, Oxford: Oxford University Press

Koolhaas, R., Foster, N. and Mendini, A. (2001) *Colours*, Blaricum: V&K Publishing

Kress, G. and Van Leeuwen, T (2001) *Multimodal Discourse – the modes and media of contemporary communication*, London: Arnold

Kress, G. and Van Leeuwen, T. (2002) 'Colour as a semiotic mode: notes for a grammar of colour', *Visual Communication* 1(3): 343-69

Kress, G. and Van Leeuwen, T. (2006) *Reading Images: the grammar of visual design*, 2nd edition, London: Routledge

Kristeva, J. (1980) *Desire in Language – a semiotic approach to language and art*, Oxford: Blackwell

Küppers, H. (1991) *Schule der Farben – Grundzüge der Farbentheorie für Computeranwende und andere*, Köln: Dumont Verlag

Lacy, M.L. (1996) *The Power of Colour to Heal the Environment*, London: Rainbow Bridge Publications

Lakoff, G. and Johnson, M. (1980) *Metaphors We Live By*, Chicago, IL: Chicago University Press

Lancôme (2010) http://www.lancome-usa.com/makeup/lipcolor/color-fever-lipstick.htm (accessed 12 February, 2010)

Lazar-Meyn, H.A. (2006) 'Colour terms in Nova Scotia', in C.P. Biggam and C.J. Kay (eds) *Progress in Colour Studies, Volume I, Language and Culture*, Amsterdam: John Benjamins, pp. 146–57

Le Corbusier (1987a[1925]) *The Decorative Arts of Today*, Cambridge, MA: MIT Press

Le Corbusier (1987b) *Journey to the East*, Cambridge, MA: MIT Press

Lewison, J. (2002) *Looking at Barnett Newman*, London: August

Ling, Y., Hurlbert, A. and Robinson, L. (2006) 'Sex Differences in Colour Preference', in N.J. Pitchford and C.P. Biggam (eds) *Progress in Colour Studies, Vol II, Psychological Aspects*, Amsterdam, John Benjamins, pp. 173–88

Lucy, J.A. (1997) 'The Linguistics of "Colour"', in C.L. Hardin and L. Maffi (eds) *Colour Categories in Thought and Language*, Cambridge: Cambridge University Press, pp. 320–46

Lupton, E. (2004) *Thinking with Type*, New York: Princeton Architectural Press

Machin, D. and Van Leeuwen, T. (2007) *Global Media Discourse – a critical introduction*, London: Routledge

MacKeigan, T. and Muth, S.Q. (2006) 'A Grammatical Network of Tzotzil-Mayan Colour Terms', in C.P. Biggam and C.J. Kay (eds) *Progress in Colour Studies, Volume I, Language and Culture*, Amsterdam: John Benjamins, pp. 25–36

Malinowski, B. (1935) *Coral Gardens and their Magic*, London: Allan and Unwin

Martín, R.M. and Ellis, M. (2001) *Pasos I*, London: Hodder and Stoughton

Matisse, H. (1972) *Matisse on Art*, London: Phaidon

Mercedes-Benz (2010) http://www.mirru.com/alubeam_chrome_paint_mercedes_benz_cl-65.htm/ (accessed 12 February 2010)

Mijksenaar, P. (20005) 'Kleur in ons dagelijks leven', *Raster* 111–12: 70–8

Mora, C. (2009) *Colour in Fashion*, Singapore: Maomao Publications

Moszynska, A. (1990) *Abstract Art*, London: Thames and Hudson

Munsell, A.H. (1969) *A Grammar of Color*, New York: Van Nostrand Reinhold

Newman, B. (1990) *Selected Writings and Interviews*, Berkeley and Los Angeles: University of California Press

O'Halloran, K. (2005) *Mathematical Discourse: language, symbolism and visual images*, London: Continuum

O'Halloran, K. (2008) 'Systemic functional multimodal discourse analysis (SF-MDA): constructing ideational meaning using language and visual imagery', *Visual Communication* 7(4): 443–77

Overy, P. (2001) *De Stijl*, London: Thames and Hudson

Painter, C. (2009) 'The Role of Colour in Children's Picture Books: Choices in AMBIENCE', in L. Unsworth (ed.) *New Literacies and the English Curriculum*, London: Continuum, pp. 89–111

Panofsky, E. (1971) *Early Netherlandish Painting*, New York: Harper & Row

Pastoureau, M. (2001) *Blue – the history of a colour*, Princeton NJ: Princeton University Press.

Pastoureau, M. (2004) *Heraldry – its origins and meaning*, London: Thames and Hudson

Pastoureau, M. (2007) *Dictionaire des couleurs de notre temps: Symbolique et société*, Paris: Editions du Seuil

Pastoureau, M. (2008) *Black – the history of a colour*, Princeton NJ: Princeton University Press

Pickford, R.W. (1972) *Psychology and Visual Aesthetics*, London: Hutchinson International

Plümacher, M. (2007) 'Color perception, color description and metaphor', in M. Plümacher and P. Holz (eds) *Speaking of Colors and Odors*, Amsterdam: John Benjamins, pp. 61–85

Riley, C.A. (1995) *Colour Codes – modern theories of color in philosophy, painting and architecture, literature, music and psychology*, Hanover: University Press of New England

Schafer, R.M. (1986) *The Thinking Ear*, Toronto: Arcana Editions

Scott-Taylor, J. (1935) *A Simple Explanation of the Ostwald Colour System*, London: Winsor and Newton

Shweder, R. and Bourne, E. (1984) 'Does the concept of the person vary cross-culturally?' in R. Schweder and R.A. Levine (eds) *Culture Theory – essays on mind, self and emotion*, Cambridge: Cambridge University Press, pp. 97–140

Smith, C. (2005) *Photoshop and Dreamweaver Interaction – creating high-impact web pages*, New York: McGraw-Hill/Osborne

Sontag, S. (1979) *Illness as Metaphor*, London: Allen Lane

Stiles, W.S. and Wyszecki, G. (2000) *Colour Science*, New York: John Wiley and Sons

THAI (2010) 'Public Information Centre: Thai Logo' http://www.thaiair.info/tips/h1013e.htm (accessed 26 March 2010)

Van Gogh, V. (1978) *The Complete Letters of Vincent van Gogh, Vol. III*, London: Thames and Hudson

Van Leeuwen, T. (1999) *Speech, Music, Sound*, London: Macmillan

Van Leeuwen, T. (2005) *Introducing Social Semiotics*, London: Routledge

Van Leeuwen, T. (2006) 'Semiotic Theory and Semiotic Practice', in M. Amano (ed.) *Multimodality – towards the most efficient communication by humans*, Nagayo: Nagayo University School of Letters, pp. 17–29

Whorf, B. (1993[1956]) *Language, Thought and Reality*, Cambridge, MA: MIT Press

Wierzbicka, A. (1996) *Semantics – primes and universals*, Oxford: Oxford University Press

Wierzbicka, A. (2006) 'The Semantics of Colour – A New Paradigm', in C.P. Biggam and C.J. Kay (eds) *Progess in Colour Studies, Volume 1: Language and Culture*, Amsterdam: Benjamins, pp. 1–24

Williams, R. (1974) *Television, Technology and Cultural Form*, London: Fontana

Wittgenstein, L. (1978) *Some Remarks About Colour*, Cambridge: Blackwell

Wyler, S. (2006) 'Colour terms between elegance and beauty', in M. Plümacher and P. Holz (eds) *Speaking of Colors and Odors*, Amsterdam: John Benjamins, pp. 113–28

Index

LIBRARY, UNIVERSITY OF CHESTER